LEITHERS

ONE FAMILY

WILLIAM HADDOW

Published 2020 CamusStone Press

ISBN 978-1-5272-6255-3

Edited by Paula Beaton - Wordnerdcopy.com

Cover design by Richie Cumberlidge - Morevisual Ltd

FOR HEATHER AND CALLUM

Contents

Authors Note/Acknowledgements

Leith has an incredible history.

This novel is a work of fiction. However, every attempt has been made to provide historical accuracy. Numerous sources have been used including *The Port of Leith* (2003) by Sue Mowet, which offers a detailed and comprehensive history of the town. Earlier volumes *The Life and Times of Leith* (Marshall, 1986) *Leith and its Antiquities* (Irons, 1897) and *History of Leith* (Campbell, 1827) have also proven invaluable.

Many websites have also provided background. Electric Scotland, Lost Edinburgh and Leith Historical Society, to name but a few, but also many, many others covering everything from medieval clothing to sailing ship design, the reformation, foodstuffs through the ages and more. A thanks also to the 'Spirit of Leith' and 'I Love Leith' Facebook groups whose members have at times provided useful points of detail. Without all the above this novel would not have been possible.

Together these have been used to help give an insight into the town's at times traumatic history (please note that the novel contains some adult themes) along with information on its many industries through the centuries: shipping, glassmaking, whisky, lead, rope making and whaling (the place must have stunk for centuries due to the boiling process), as well as its long history of shipbuilding.

With a few exceptions all characters are fictional. However, a special mention has to go to *Past lives of Leith* (Franklin, Troy, Britton, Wilson, Lawson, 2019) which offers a detailed account of the bodies exhumed from Constitution Street as part of the tram construction process. Through the use of facial reconstruction, we can see that these people looked as we do. A few of these individuals appear in some of the stories.

To fit with the concept of the book on a few occasions I have compressed into one 24-hour period incidents that may have happened over several days or even weeks.

Other than that, any errors are my own and if you spot any, please forgive them and accept this as the (occasionally dark) love letter to Leith it is intended to be.

Bill Haddow

June 2020

Notes

Geography

In the period covered in the early part of this this novel the shoreline at Leith would have been roughly in line with Bernard Street/Commercial street (the Kings Wark would have been close to the water's edge). As the port developed, more and more land was reclaimed to build the dock area.

Sandport Street was the original water line of the river. Land reclamation has narrowed it considerably.

Place names

Apart from in the early chapters, modern street names are used.

In the first five chapters:

St Leonards Lands is now known as Coalhill.

The High Street is now known as Tolbooth Wynd.

Rotten Row is now known as Water Street.

Hie Gait is now known as Sandport Street.

Chapter 1

The Lands

The Road to Leith - 15th October 1364

John had kissed him. Peter shuddered at the thought.

Black clumsy clouds darkened way to the north. The air now cooler, the wind strengthening.

The monks had come from their precinct at Holyrood, up over the Abbey Hill and past the quarries. There was a scrunch of pebbles as the pair made their way down the eastern road, their destination the Abbey's holdings at the mouth of the river at Inverleith.

To either side of the track lay open moorland. Thickets of gorse, broom, and occasional woodland. A few sheep and cattle grazed. The odd person gathering wood and signs that peats had been dug along the edge of the path. In the few sheltered spots lay strips of ploughed land among a scattering of isolated wooden or earth walled cottages.

At first glance, the monks appeared to be wearing the same black robes. Closer inspection would have shown that the older man, stooped, white-haired and with an ambling gait, wore a superior quality woollen habit with a cowl hood over his cassock. A substantial gold cross on a chain around his neck and on his finger a beautiful ring, a large sapphire, the symbol of heaven.

The younger man led the packhorse. Tall and gangly, his fair hair styled in a monk's tonsure, clean-shaven in the centre of his scalp. A red rash of pimples covered his square jaw, a contrast with his pale blue eyes.

Young Peter was yet unaware of the surprises in store for him later that day. They would set off a chain of events, the effects of which would leave an imprint far into the future. Now, he had other concerns; his face carried a haunted look.

Peter had to admit to himself, whatever angle he looked from there was no getting away from it. He was both confused and troubled by what happened. In the stables yesterday his good friend, Canon John, had kissed him. From that moment onwards his stomach had been churning.

Last night he had tried praying. No answers came. He couldn't think of anyone to ask. Certainly not old Canon Anderson with him now. He had been a novice monk only a few weeks; it was too much.

The older monk ambled along. He was oblivious of Peter's concerns, his red face animated despite the heavy rings round his sagging eyes.

"Look around lad, what do you see? A few people scraping a living from the land, riven with superstition. Along this road, we will find a few fisherfolks with the folk from the harbour." He continued on at the same steady pace. "We bring these people prayer and knowledge of the Lord's works. Without our teachings, those residing here would be barbarians. What you need to understand is that what our Abbey brings is beyond value. There is little commerce and industry that happens outside our walls. Only some farming and fishing, and it's the only place a lad like you…" He stopped to put his hood up against the wind, glanced across at Peter. His eyes narrowed. "And if you don't get that sour look off your face, you'll feel my hand across it," he snapped. He paused and continued, "…can get an education. Our Abbey has blossomed over the years and not only do we have our library and scriptorium but we now have brothers who are experts in many vital subjects. Farming, building, learning."

Old Canon Anderson was Peter's mentor. A grumpy though not unpleasant old man, Peter suspected he was often drunk. His job was to explain to Peter his role as a cellular assistant ensuring food supplies, and also the customs and purpose of the Abbey. Old Anderson was very serious about his role. Peter soon realised that the best policy was to just listen. If he ever asked a question, Canon Anderson ignored it and would continue with whatever subject he happened to be on. This journey like many before thus involved Peter walking in silence while Anderson rarely stopped talking.

As they came down the slope, the wind freshened. Peter became aware of the salt in the cold air; he could both see and hear the wide Firth up ahead. He sighed as they continued on their way. He usually paid attention to what the old man told him but today he was distracted.

He couldn't stop himself going over the incident in the stables. John was a few years older and had befriended him when he arrived from his village in the Borders a few short weeks before. With Peter being the fifth son of a smallholder, a career in the church had seemed the best option. Where he came from most people wouldn't travel more than a few miles from their home for an entire lifetime. The Abbey offered something better.

John had kissed him. It was such a shock. *What should he do about it?* When he had analysed it afterwards what had he felt? *Had it aroused him? Or did he imagine that?*

"Over to the right is the links." Anderson gestured towards the large expanse of scrub and sand hillocks with the odd clump of grass which stretched onwards until it reached the beach and the water's edge. "That's common land."

A wave of weariness came over Peter. From the moment he had arrived at the Abbey there was little spare time given the constant rounds of work, prayers, and classes. What little time he had he spent in the chambers he shared with the other novices. Here the gossip was rife. Those mysteries that were new to Peter.

Girls, boys, sex, it was all so confusing. He had heard the rumours that some older monks flouted the rules of chastity and had sexual relations with each other. Even that some senior monks had female concubines outside the Abbey walls. Peter was also very aware that they had received a lecture only the other week on the Devil's work in relation to this subject. The church's teachings were very clear.

Peter experienced a surge of despair. His head swam. He shuddered. *What should he do?* The confusion continued to spin around in his mind. He was glad that old Anderson had a rare period of silence as they navigated a boggy section of the track. They turned northwards towards the river of Leith.

The wide expanse of clear water meandered towards the sea, patches of reeds on either side at the bottom of the grassy sloping bank becoming steeper as it met the narrow pebble beach at its edge.

"Over there, the little hamlet of North Leith," said Anderson, pointing. "The whole bank of the river on that side belongs to our Abbey and the fisherfolk living in that cluster of cottages; their job is to provide us with fish. And your job," he said, stabbing Peter in the chest with an unfriendly grin, "is to collect them and make sure everyone stumps up."

The old canon then stopped and spread his hands.

"Where we are standing now is the St Leonards Lands. The Abbey owns this strip of the bank along this side, also the few cottages and warehouses you can see." He swung his wizened frame around forty-five degrees and pointed towards the sea. "Further down this side of the riverbank is the land of Sir Robert Logan. He lives in the big village up at Restalrig in his castle. He's built a parish church up there and he owns everything else on this side and much more besides."

There was little activity at present. A few small craft tied along the riverside and others dragged up onto the sloping bank. Towards the sea two larger ones swung and creaked in the strengthening wind, their anchors brought across and secured to trees on the shore.

A few earthen walled cottages interspersed the trees that lined the bank at the top of the slope. Outside one a young woman came and threw a wooden bucket of scraps into the water. A pair of squabbling seagulls swooped. At another, a boat builder worked on a repair to the bottom of a small fishing skiff. There was a whiff of rotting carcass from behind the local flesher's house.

"It looks quiet now and, in some ways, it's a backwater," said Anderson. "For a long time it's been an important place for bringing and sending goods. The English have occupied on several occasions."

Peter feigned interest. He gave an impression of listening but his mind kept wandering, reliving the embrace with John.

"Although now we are at peace and we hope that kind of thing is in the past. There's what, mmm … around twenty-five big ships a year come and go. Some of these are the Abbeys. They bring in many kinds of luxuries such as wine, linen, and spices and going the other direction it's wool and hides most of the time." Canon Anderson then pointed to a boat sitting close by at the river's edge. "You see that boat with the wide bottom by the river? That's the ferry; the ferryman will take you and the horse across. Our Abbey owns that too."

As they made their way to the water's edge the Ferryman looked up and shouted, "You need to be quick, there's a storm coming."

Canon Anderson looked north at the mounting dark clouds, the wind now increased in strength. The rain started to spatter down.

"Take the horse to the cottages over the river and collect their fish. Offer blessings and prayers to any who request it," he looked again at the darkening skies. "I'll be offering guidance to the folk by the other warehouses on Lord Logan's land. His Lordship is a friend of the church."

Peter knew that this meant it was likely that Canon Anderson would sit getting drunk while he had to do the work. He knew he should have been angry, but with all the emotions swirling in his head it would be unwise to add more.

"Get on your way," said Anderson as he turned and started to walk towards the river's mouth. "Oh, and stop at the Preston's cottage, it's the first one. His daughter is ill, and he wants you to offer prayers. Mr Preston is a regular at the services at the Abbey, and we wouldn't want to disappoint him."

As the boat set off on the short crossing Peter mulled over his first few weeks. A novice monk's life was hard work. But there were also many good things. Different trades and the chance of an education. There was security here. A life that was better than the backbreaking drudgery of his father's farmstead.

Now this incident with Brother John had turned everything upside down. John was a fully-fledged monk as he himself would be if he worked hard over the next few years. After the kiss yesterday, Peter had pushed him away and scurried to the chapel for prayers. Peter knew he had felt something. He just wasn't sure what.

Peter led the horse off the ferry just as the ferocity of the wind and rain increased. He made his way up the muddy track to the cluster of cottages. The people of South Leith's local parish church was at the much larger village at Restalrig. For the handful of fisherfolk of North Leith, the only option was the long journey to Holyrood. For that reason, few of them attended. Mr Preston was an exception; Peter knew he was a deeply religious man and rarely missed a service at the Abbey on the Sabbath.

The storm had started in earnest; a biting wind whipped Peter's habit around his legs as the rain became a deluge. He ran for the first cottage, knocked on the door of wicker rods. It opened with a slow creak. A powerful smell of rotten fish and manure hit Peter. Mr Preston stood there, saying nothing. With his one good eye (the other had a squint) he looked at Peter with a penetrating, suspicious stare. He was a tall man, well built with thick muscular arms protruding from a filthy smock. His hair was lank and his large, round face unshaven. He moved his face close; Peter caught a whiff of stale breath.

Mr Preston then scanned the worsening weather, turned back to Peter and in a slow deep voice he said, "Our God comes and does not keep silence; a fire devours before him, and round about him a mighty tempest rages."

He turned back into the house. Peter stood, nonplussed, uncertain what to do. By now he was soaked.

A young woman came to the door. She was a comely lass, sweet-faced and with that shy look young women often wear, a typical country girl. Well built under her woollen smock, her long dark hair tied back. She introduced herself as Mary and in a soft voice said, "Come on in out of that terrible weather. I'll see to your horse."

Peter was ushered into the house, relieved to be out of the worsening storm.

The cottage comprised one large room with a cooking fire at one end with a hole in the roof for the smoke. In front of the fire was a pallet bed in which lay a sick girl aged about ten. Against one wall two beds of heather, and against the other a rough table and a wooden chest. The earthen floor was spread with rushes. At the other end of the house the floor was covered in animal dung and a few goats now shared their space with Peter's horse. A flimsy wall made of rushes separated the animals from the living space. All around the house were stores of various fishing paraphernalia, nets, hooks, baskets of bait.

Sadness crossed Marys face.

"This is Beatrice; she has the flux."

Peter crossed himself as he approached the girl's bedside. Mr Preston and Mary then knelt down by the bed. Peter stood. The father gestured to Peter to kneel. He did. With a nod Preston said, "Let us pray."

There was silence. Mr Preston then again looked at Peter with his intense one-eyed stare.

Peter stuttered, "A … a … almighty and eternal God, you are the everlasting health of those who believe in you. Hear us for your sick servant Beatrice, for whom we implore the aid of your tender mercy. Let her be restored to bodily health, so she may give thanks to you in your church. Through Christ our Lord."

And so, it began. It soon became clear to Peter that this would be a long session.

For the next two hours they took turns at praying. Mostly Mr Preston, at times Mary and often Peter to the extent that he had soon run out of options and was having to repeat the limited number of prayers he knew, some for the third or fourth time. Outside the storm continued to rage, and the wind whistled through the gaps around the door.

Peter's knees were hurting as darkness fell. He was relieved when Mr Preston, at last, stood. Then as Peter made to follow, Preston turned, moved close to him and said with a hiss, "Do not contaminate thy daughter, causing her to commit fornication, lest the land be prostituted, and the land become full of wickedness."

There was a long pause, then he slowly enunciated, "Leviticus nineteen, verse twenty-nine." Preston then turned and looked at Mary on her knees. He turned back to Peter who was flummoxed; he couldn't fathom what this meant. Mr Preston was a strange man. Preston then threw him a filthy woollen blanket and gestured that he should follow him to the barn end of the house.

"You can't travel in the dark in this weather." He gestured to the other end of the room. "Sleep over there."

There was a pause. This was the first time Mr Preston had talked to him without referring to the scriptures. Preston turned to him again and thrust his face to within inches of his, giving Peter a nose full of foul breath.

"I lie down and sleep; I wake again because the Lord sustains me."

For a time, Peter lay in the darkness and his mind spun. Collecting fish, the Abbey gossip, Mr Preston, John's kiss, prayers. *What did it mean…?* He struggled to put any coherent thoughts together until at last, he fell asleep on the bed of hay next to the horse and goats.

He woke up with a start, disorientated at first. The wind was still howling outside, but it was pitch dark; he realised it must be the middle of the night.

A small flame appeared on the other side of the flimsy divide. Candlelight flickered. The light moved towards him until he saw it was Mary, wrapped in a grey woollen cloak.

"Mary, what the…" He sat up.

Mary knelt down to put her hand on his chest, moved her mouth towards his and gave him a gentle kiss. Peter experienced a mixture of shock and pleasure, every nerve in his body alert.

"B … but Mary, your father," spluttered Peter as quietly as he could.

She paused and cocked her head to listen. Loud snoring came from the other end of the house.

She then whispered in his ear, "The Lord God fashioned into a woman the rib which he had taken from the man and brought her to the man."

Mary then let her cloak drop to the floor to reveal her naked, healthy, plump white body. Peter gasped at the clear sight of it in the candlelight.

In one quick movement Mary then grabbed the hem of his habit and pulled it roughly over his head. She brought her face close to his, looked him straight in the eyes and whispered, "For indeed man was not created for the woman's sake, but woman for the man's sake."

She pushed him onto the hay and lay down beside him, his skin tingling as their bodies made contact. Peter looked up at the heather-covered rafters, thick with spiders' webs. For a full ten seconds, he thought about the lecture on this very subject. It had only been the week before. He tried to remember the details.

Sex was not permitted on any of the feast days. Not during advent or Whitsun week or Easter week. Not within the church walls and not for the eight days leading to a woman's husband taking the Eucharist. He wracked his brains; there was much more, but he couldn't remember. The thoughts became a jumble.

Peter turned to her and returned her embrace. He took a sharp intake of breath at the gorgeous warmth of her ample breasts on his chest. He groaned. Peter realised that things were now clear. There was no confusion; his body's reaction told him everything. He pulled himself on top of her, on his face the expression of a man who had unexpectedly discovered a large pot of gold.

Historical Note

King David I founded Holyrood Abbey in 1128 and much of what is now Leith came under its control. Responsibility was shared with the Lords Logan, who by 1351 had gained the lands from a Lord Lasteric (who gave his name to the village of Restalrig and whose family had likely come across with William the Conqueror.)

We now know St Leorards Lands as Coalhill

Chapter 2

The Betrayal

The Shore, Leith – 3rd September 1398

Agnes Preston took advantage of the brief gap in custom. With her quick, agile step, she popped back past the warehouses that lined the Shore. The cottage sat with a handful of others, near the entrance to the Firth. A small cluster of scruffy hovels. The lower courses made from boulders from the beach, bound with hot lime. Gaps filled with earth divots and thatched with a mixture of heather and reeds.

Agnes had gone home to make sure her sister was managing with the older children. After checking all was well, she stepped out the door to return to the tavern. She almost bumped into Tam, her sister's husband. Agnes immediately knew that something was wrong. Tam was a lean and taught little man, not an ounce of fat on him from his work on the fishing boats. His wiry body and bald head contrasted with Agnes' long dark hair and willowy frame. Tam was a man of few words but on this occasion, he looked genuinely distressed; he appeared breathless, as if he had been running.

He stuttered in haste to get the words out.

"A … Ag … Agnes I've something important to tell you."

She led him away from the cottages to the riverside.
"What is it, Tam?"

"I… I was dragging my boat up when I met Wallace, you know, his Lordship's man who works down here sometimes."

Tam paused, regaining his breath.
"And?" said Agnes, unable to contain her irritation.
"Well, he says that Lord Logan has sold the Shore to Edinburgh." Tam's eyes were wide with concern.

Agnes felt a jolt of adrenaline course through her. Her whole body juddered. She stood open-mouthed.

"Wh … what?" She staggered a step back. "That can't be true."
Tam shook his head. "Wallace is not the type to make up such a thing."

Agnes took her time coming back along the riverbank, her mind in turmoil. Although a bright sunny day, she pulled her long brown woollen belted tunic tight around her as if cold.

She stopped to sit on a large boulder to think. Looking across the wide river mouth, the fast current checked at low tide as it approached the Firth. The silt that accumulated along the banks narrowed the stream and formed a sand bar at its mouth; larger boats could only cross at high tide.

There was a ship today; a substantial flat bottom Cog from Danzig arrived on the morning tide. It sat near the middle of the river, the anchor loaded into one of the small local craft and rowed to the water's edge. A group of sailors were now securing it to a tree above the beach with an array of ropes. Unloading into smaller boats would begin over the next few days. A relay brought the cargo of spice, soap, flax and timber and delivered it on the Shore's wooden quayside. Later the ship would be filled with wool and salted fish and travel the other way.

Agnes entered the tavern just as her husband Richard was pushing two drunken Dutch mariners through the wide doorway out onto the street. It wasn't yet noon. The smell was of ale, horse manure and male sweat. Her head was in a spin; she didn't know if she could bring herself to tell him.

"Time to go, gentlemen, your captain will need you," Richard said firmly as he slammed the door behind them. He crossed the room to the big chair near the bar and sat his large frame down with a sigh. He was a big man with an athletic build, ruddy complexion and an unruly mop of fair hair.

"Another busy morning," said Agnes.

"Aye, hard work but it's going well. Couldn't have as fine a living if we were still doing the fishing."

William, the youngest of his four children had climbed into his arms. Richard sat back contented, happy to get a minute's break and aware there would be a stream of customers arriving soon.

Agnes said nothing and went behind the bar and kept herself busy rinsing mugs used for serving ale. Some a rough earthenware, others made of leather and waterproofed with beeswax.

She could remember her auld grannie telling her that her grandad and his father before him, and even his father before him had always worked the boats on this river. This river was her home. Her people had always been here. Much of her family now still worked them, although a few worked in the group of long wooden tofts that lined the Shore, the warehouses owned by the church or rich merchants.

She knew they were lucky that Lord Logan had given Richard and her permission to set up their little tavern. It wasn't much, but they had spent a long time making it the best they could and they paid him a good rent for it. Agnes had hoped that their venture would set them up for life and that they'd have something to hand onto their children. That now seemed in danger. She brought a wicker broom out from behind the bar.

"You're a good father to our bairns," she said as she swept a pile of old rushes across the floor. They created a billowing cloud as along with horse manure and mud she forcefully swept them out the door.

"Some men would pay no attention to them; never ceases to surprise me given that you never knew your own."

"No, I never found out who my father was, my mam wouldn't tell me," said Richard. He looked thoughtful. "I'd asked her several times, tried to get it out of her in the days before she died but by then she was away with the fairies. Was always a religious woman. She started to babble on about the bible and stormy nights and it all being God's work. The jabbering of a mad old woman, so we'll never know."

The clip clop of a long train of packhorses was heard streaming onto the Shore. Experience told them that the drovers would soon fill their little wooden tavern and demand the ale they brewed in the outhouse at the back.

Richard stood and looked across at Agnes. He frowned. "Is there anything the matter?"

*

Custom varied with the seasons. Trains of packhorses heaped with wool from all over the east of Scotland arrived in the autumn. Soon the barns and warehouses would be full with their goods ready for export. In spring it was cowhides as most of the slaughtering was in November for Michaelmas. Other custom came from locals and mariners, their ships bringing imports of olive oil, wine, linen, canvas, sugar, saffron, pepper, and everything in between for the market in Edinburgh.

As expected, the tavern was soon busy, the few spartan wooden tables occupied with the usual mixture of packhorse drovers, carters, sailors, local fishers and various tradesmen. Coopers, Sawyers and the Blacksmith. There was more trade than a small village would normally expect because of the port.

The atmosphere was different from earlier that morning. Agnes paced in a rage, her face a beetroot red.

"I can't believe it's true. That horrible little money grabber. We are his vassals for goodness' sake," she hissed, ugly hot tears welling in her eyes. "Lord Logan has a duty towards us; we spend our lives serving him and in return, he should look after us."

She slammed a large pitcher of foaming ale on the bar. The carter who had ordered it, seeing her expression said nothing and moved sheepishly back to his table.

"But no, that nasty little man sold the Shore to Edinburgh and with it will go our livelihood, just so he can go on living in his castle at Lochend and go swanning off down south for his stupid jousting."

Richard stood, his face pale as if still in shock. "How long do you think we have?"

Not long I expect; I'll bet you that fat Baillie McTavish will arrive here soon with his great slimy pockmarked face," she replied with a scowl. "He must have known this was coming. I thought he was looking at our place enviously. These Edinburgh Burgesses will have it off us as soon as you like."

Richard said nothing but groaned, struggling with his anger.

Soon afterwards there was a commotion outside. A murmur went around as Baillie McTavish made his entrance. An unpopular, pompous, beefy man with a fat neck, his whole demeanour smug, he radiated his sense of entitlement. His jowls wobbled as he waddled up to the bar, dressed up like a peacock in a quality red wool coat and a black wide-brimmed hat with a feather. He stood with his usual sneering smile.

"Ah, Mr and Mrs Preston, I come bearing news that I'm sure will interest you."

To Richard's amazement, Agnes smiled demurely. The Baillie manoeuvred his great frame onto a corner stool. He had trouble squeezing in his enormous belly which strained against the tabletop. His wispy beard struggled to disguise the bad skin on his podgy face, his eyes puffy and heavy-lidded.

"But first I must partake in some of your finest fare. Pottage and a piece of your best meat pie if you please and a tankard of your finest ale."

Agnes played the part of a dutiful innkeeper, making small talk and smiling at the fat Baillie's feeble attempts at humour. Richard meanwhile stood behind the bar serving the other customers, seething and having difficulty not to show it; he couldn't believe that his wife could treat this man with any civility. Once he had finished eating the Baillie rose and moved to the centre of the room.

"Now for my news," he pulled a piece of paper out of his pocket, opened it with a flourish and started to read.

"Starting today, the good Burgesses of Edinburgh have rights over all goods coming in and out of the Shore." He leered at Agnes and then gloated at Richard.

"And you know fine well that Lord Logan owns this land," shouted a carter in the corner. "You Burgesses have the right to land your goods here, nothing more."

"Ha, that's where you are wrong," shouted the Baillie with a snarl through his cracked teeth. "The good people of Edinburgh have bought the rights from your Lord Logan and it's us that now own the Shore."

He then pointed his podgy thumb at himself and with a satisfied sneer said, "And given I'm the Baillie here it means that that you are answerable to me. If in doubt, go ask your Lord; we will soon see who is boss around here."

He turned to Agnes with an evil smile and shook his fat finger at her. "There's going to be changes here, let me tell you. As for your tavern Mrs Preston, without permission of the Edinburgh Burgesses these premises are illegal, and we frown on it." He turned and looked around the tavern. "I've heard what you get up to here what with your gaming, your smuggling, and, I'll wager prostitution." He looked directly at Agnes.

Richard, his face angry at the insult made to come from behind the bar but Agnes stood in front of him barring his way.

"I can think of someone who would do an excellent job running this place." He waddled towards the door. "Yes. My nephew, I think."

He stopped and turned at the doorway.

"I'll give you until tomorrow to clear out back to your hovel. Your family are fishermen not tavern owners; get back to where you belong."

Richard pushed past Agnes and slammed the door so hard it made the whole building shake.

"Fat bastard," he shouted. "Aargh, how I would love to get at that slob."

Agnes stood leaning on the bar with a smirk on her face.

Richard turned, rage in his eyes. "How can you stand there smiling given what he's done to us?"

"I pissed in his ale, his pie I made from that rat I killed in the cellar this morning. The pottage contained enough herbs to make sure the Baillie will be running to sit on the pot every hour for the next week." Agnes grinned. "I don't think fat Baillie McTavish will visit anyone for a while."

*

That night was moonless. In the pitch dark several small craft were quietly dragged down the beach and into the river. It was a short row out to the anchored Cog. Under the ship's single light, payment was made by the Leith men to the watchman. Over the next few hours they relayed half the cargo across the river and hid it in the tiny fishing hamlet of North Leith.

"They can own us but they won't be getting any duty on all that stuff," whispered Richard.

The Leithers then rowed their boats home, dragged them up onto the beach and secured them in their usual place. They crept back up to their cottages.

"I've one more thing I have to do, Richard, I'll be back soon," said Agnes as she slipped into the darkness.

Agnes prised open the back door of the tavern and crept inside. She took one final look at what they had built and put so much of their life into. She stuck the flint and a small flame appeared in the dry grass she had brought with her. She set a fire behind a barrel. By the time she had returned to her cottage, she was able to turn and watch her dreams of a better life go up in flames.

Historical Note

In 1398 Lord Logan sold his feudal rights and granted the Burgh of Edinburgh a wide-ranging charter which gave them full ownership of the strip of land on the south-eastern bank (now known as the Shore). Logan also renounced his right to keep taverns in Leith "for the sale of wine or shops for merchandise or to grind bread for sale". Edinburgh had paid well for its new rights.

Sir Robert Logan's sale of his feudal rights to Edinburgh was to bring trouble for the inhabitants of Leith for many centuries to come.

The high-water mark at this time was roughly in line with where Commercial and Bernard Street are now.

In the 14th and 15th centuries, much of Europe operated with a "burgh system", a form of monopoly gifted to a town by the sovereign to enable the officials and Burgesses of the burgh (who had to live within its walls) to control trade and set standards. Foreign trade, in particular, was fiercely protected from outsiders.

A Baillie was an official of the Burgh.

Chapter 3

The Preceptory

St Anthony's, Leith – 28th October 1434

"**A**nd you will leave this place and return to Holyrood at once!" screamed Canon Daumont, so close that a spray of spittle covered the young monk's face.

The novice quaked.

"We can do without your sort here; you will be gone by this afternoon."

The Canon about-turned, his black cassock flapping and face fuming as he moved from the hallway back into the administration chamber. The door slammed shut.

The two aged monks huddled together in the corner made sure they did nothing but appear to be concentrating on the books on their table. They'd been at St Anthony's long enough to know that to cross Canon Daumont was unwise. His tantrums were not only reserved for those enthusiastic young newcomers who challenged the status quo. They knew that while this man could be utterly charming when he wanted to be, he was also pompous and full of his own self-importance. Along with the other monks and staff at the hospital they toiled to do their best to care for their sick residents. They were aware that Daumont had absolutely no sympathy, or empathy or even any interest in those they cared for other than to pilfer from them anything of value (including the beautiful large sapphire ring he always wore on his left hand).

Canon Daumont glared in their direction before moving to sit on the handsome carved chair at his desk. He quivered with anger. With a beaky nose and greying temples, his small piercing eyes narrowed at the pile of parchments on his desk. Daumont took a deep breath to help his rage subside; he didn't experience many emotions other than this one.

*

In the four years he had been at sea, the past week was by far the worst weather Robert Preston had experienced. In early October it turned nasty with storms all along the coast; at least two shipwrecks from what they had been told. A Hulk carrying wine and spices had gone down with all hands off Dunbar while a Cog full of hides out of Leith had been blown across the Forth before running aground and breaking up on Aberdour beach. The good news was that Rob's own cargo might now get a higher price.

Rob slumped against the mast, his wind scorched face and cracked lips showing both relief and exhaustion as the curved shape of his big Hulk the "Helena" limped past the black rocks at the river mouth to the safety of the harbour. They just made it over the sandbar on an ebbing tide.

Rob experienced a wave of happiness; so good to see the familiar quay at the Shore. Some things were changed. A large new tower now guarded the mouth of the estuary, the Kings Wark. A more substantial stone wall and paving added at the quayside. The same collection of wooden warehouses interspersed with a few clusters of cottages with heather thatch huddled together among the trees that lined the top of the river's sloping bank. Rob looked upriver, impressed and surprised by the fine curved arches of the new stone bridge that spanned it, where in the past there had been only a ferry.

A haar shrouded the village as the Helena caught a damp breeze and glided to a berth at St Leonards Lands. Robert and his crew looked like men who had been through an ordeal. Tall and broad, Robert's long straggly fair hair framed a high brow, his eyes salt red; a thick beard covered his square jaw. Barefoot, his woollen pullover and knee-length breeches were in tatters.

The Helena had sustained significant damage, the single sail ripped in several places and the main mast cracked; the remaining crew aware they were lucky to be alive. Last week's dangers had brought home the tenuous link between life and death. A young man in his prime, it was his determination that saw him through. Two crewmen had been less fortunate and gone over the side during the worst of the storms.

*

Although a small institution compared to the Abbey, the Preceptory of St Anthony still had an important role and Canon Daumont struggled to understand why his superiors didn't see how difficult it was with such useless staff under him. He ran a tight ship and believed in efficiency. It was important that everyone understood that. Not only did St Anthony's have to care for the sick and old (not that he would ever demean himself by dirtying his hands with that sort of thing) but it operated orchards, farm, gardens, livestock, a graveyard and the chapel – in the Nave of which, unfortunately, his superiors had decided the local people could now worship. He tutted at the thought of his endless responsibilities, managing the property along with confessions, mass, burials and schooling.

He shot a disgusted glance at the cowering old monks in the corner. *I'm surrounded by fools,* he thought. Ridiculous that they expected him to operate this place with only ancient imbeciles to help. *It's a farce, and these young idiots they send me…* He really should complain to the Bishop.

Daumont again eyed the large stack of parchments waiting on his desk, his irritation increasing. The first an order for the purchase of candles and wine. With a flourish he signed. Then a bill for the repair of the orchard wall. Another for clothing for the few orphans the Preceptory took in during the recent outbreak. The orphans. There was something about the young and vulnerable that interested him; he knew this could bring another rare emotional response. He sensed a slight stiffening in his cock. *Mmmm … that little fair-haired one that had arrived a week or so back after the epidemic swept through.* He liked the look of her, pretty, a virgin most likely, Yes, that was the sort he liked. Young and defenceless. He signed the bill. At least there would be some entertainment in this god-forsaken hole; it was the least he deserved given what he had to put up with.

*

On deck Rob furled the torn sail as the crew secured the ship to the bank. He glanced up and instantly recognised his Uncle William standing on the wharf. Rob smiled. William was a small-scale merchant – he appeared well; squat, ruddy-faced with bushy sideburns and an expensive looking coat. Rob had always liked him; he knew how to laugh, ever ready with a joke or a quip. Their eyes met, and he saw the sombre look on his uncle's face. Rob's shoulders slumped; all was not well.

They visited Rob's parents' cottage. It had never been the most salubrious of places, a lowly earth walled hovel. It looked very sad now, empty and cold, with the smell of damp and decay and no fire in the hearth. There were still a few personal effects to remind him of his family: an old shirt that had belonged to his father, his mother's dented old cooking pot and a pair of well-worn wooden shoes that he knew were his younger brother's. Not much of an inheritance.

"They went quickly," said William as Robert rummaged through the few belongings. "Didn't suffer for long."

They headed towards the graveyard at the Preceptory. The river was quiet, a few small craft attached to the bank along with his own. A thin drizzle added to the depressing atmosphere, little sound other than the cry of seagulls as they swooped around the quay, a pair of swans gliding noiselessly upriver. While further up above the tree's rooks circled with raucous cries.

"It wasn't a big outbreak; it seemed to vanish just as quickly as it had arrived," said William.

Rob didn't reply, he couldn't find the words, his whole immediate family gone. Not that unusual – neighbours had suffered the same. There was no God. If there was, would he do such a thing? These priests and their stupid stories. His travels had shown him they were often corrupt and liars.

They left the cottages and warehouses behind them and made their way up the scrub covered slope where Lord Logan's lands met the land of Pilrig and the Preceptory. Three pigs snuffled in a midden, the bells around their necks, worn by pigs belonging to the Preceptory, letting out a gentle chime.

The graveyard stood some way off from St Anthony's, the custom that the shadow of the church must never rest upon the burials. Rob and William stood over the row of five new wooden crosses. William crossed himself, Rob didn't. His mother and father, his three brothers. Next to them the older crosses of those who had gone before. His two sisters who had died young, his grandparents Richard and Agnes who at one time had run a tavern on the Shore.

With a start a face flashed across Rob's mind, He shuddered. "But where's Margery?" he said looking at his uncle. "My wee sister."

William looked surprised, realising the thought hadn't crossed his mind.

"Oh, Margery, of course. I've only just returned to Leith myself; I'm told the priests took her in."

*

"Margery," Daumont said kindly, "take these candles to the Chapel and set them by the altar."

Margery took them, gave a quick bow and scurried off, her sweet face sombre.

She had been in a daze for the last week since her parents and brothers had died. Although she had carried out her tasks, helping in the hospital best she could, she was numb. At twelve years old she already knew you just had to keep going, taking it one day at a time. Everyone else here had suffered; she wasn't special.

She walked across the courtyard and entered the side door. It was quiet, only the echo from her own footsteps as she crossed to the altar. A dim light came from the small stained-glass window at the far end of the building. The sound of a lock clicking as she set the candles in their holders took her by surprise. She turned; Canon Daumont stood by the side door.

"Yes, Father?"

Daumont rushed towards her and grabbed her by the hair. Margery started to protest; her face stung as he slapped her hard. A rag in her mouth, he held her hands together and dragged and pushed her onto her back onto the front row of pews.

"You're the pretty one," he said with a leer.

With one hand still holding her hair he used the other to pull up her smock. His cock started to harden at the sight of her young white thighs, and the look of terror on her face.

"Just how I like it," he gave a cruel chuckle. "I prefer you girls who wriggle a bit."

He sensed his excitement rising as his cock fully hardened, he tore off her undergarments and thought to enter her. Then paused, sniffed. *Mmm … he liked the scent of her, he wanted to taste her.*

"What's the hurry?" he said aloud.

Daumont had planned well, making sure everyone was busy at work elsewhere in the complex and the chapel doors locked.

"Let's do this properly, let's take our time," he said. He grinned, showing cracked teeth.

Briefly releasing her he grabbed the hem of his cassock to pull it over his head. Margery was terrified by the stink of his sweat. Pinned down by her hair, she was helpless. With her sudden release, almost with a reflex action she brought her knees up to her chin. Her torso twisted as she kicked her legs out and upwards with all her might. Canon Daumont released himself from his cassock and threw himself forward to put his full naked weight upon her. There was a deep thud as Margery's heels connected with the Canon's nose with a sickening squish. Daumont's nose burst open, blood spurting as he fell backwards to the floor with a howl of pain. Margery turned and dropped off the pew onto the floor, scrabbling underneath to the row behind. The Canon made a grab with his now bloody hands, lunging for her ankle but the blood was slippery and she manged to break free.

"You little bitch," he screamed.

Margery jumped up and ran for the side door. She turned the handle. Locked.

Canon Daumont stood up, blood pouring from his nose.

"You'll pay for that," he hissed.

He strode towards her. Margery picked up a small statue of Saint Peter and hurled it at him. It glanced off the side of his head and he stumbled.

Margery ran. Daumont grasped at her but she was too quick. She ran down the aisle to the rear of the church, she threw open the door behind the altar, the Canon raging after her. At the end of the corridor, the latrine, she scrambled head first through the hole, crawled along the narrow tunnel and up the bank of the sewer ditch outside the back of the chapel.

She set off running, hearing the click of the side door lock, then the Canon's yell. She ran across to and through the kitchen, the cook shouting as she almost knocked a tray of bread out of his hands. Ran as fast as she could through the orchard. She jumped over the orchard wall. She ran through the vegetable patch.

Her fear drove her as she careered out the Preceptory gates. She tore along the path towards Leith, her heart pumping, her eyes filled with tears, running blind.

To her horror, powerful arms grabbed her. Her whole body froze; she was pinned, there was no escape.

Then Margery's heart sang.

She recognised the smell of the strong man holding her.

*

Canon Daumont rubbed his nose gingerly. He had pulled the hood of his cassock over his head to hide the swelling for prayers and then confession that evening. He had thought it might be broken, although he had spent most of the time thinking how he was going make that little trollop pay.

That evening's queue of parishioners taking confession was coming to its end.

Thank God, he thought, *here am I in agony and I've got to listen to their stupid little problems.*

"Ten hail Marys," he said.

On the other side of the divide the old woman rose and left.

"Well, praise the Lord that's over," he said aloud as he gently fingered his nose again. He made to rise but then to his surprise the seat through the thin curtain creaked as another person entered.

"Forgive me, Father, for I have sinned," said the voice.

Canon Daumont realised that the man on the other side of the screen was not one of his regular parishioners, yet the voice was local.

"Tell me my son, how long since you last took confession, how long have you been separated from the Lord's guidance?"

"Many years, Father."

That voice! He was sure he had heard it before but he couldn't quite place it.

"How have you sinned, my son?"

"I have taken the Lord's name in vain. I have lain with wenches. I have brought about the deaths of more than one."

Canon Daumont sensed a growing tension in the man's speech.

"My son, the holy sacrament of confession is not something to take lightly. For all these sins, do you ask God's forgiveness?"

"I seek penance for the sins I'm yet to commit."

Daumont felt the skin on the back of his neck prickle; something about this wasn't right. He brought his face closer to the screen and tried to peer through, but it was too dark. He could see a shape. He felt alarmed but he couldn't quite work out why. Then the sound of fabric ripping. He caught sight of a glint of metal.

The final thing the Canon heard was the gurgling of his own blood as it flooded his throat, pierced deeply by a long, thin blade. The last thing he felt was a ring being removed from his finger.

Historical Note

St Anthony's Preceptory was founded in 1430 by Lord Logan of Restalrig. Staffed by French Augustine Canons, it was a smaller religious house known as a preceptory or hospital and built as a work of Christian charity to offer shelter to the weak, old and infirm. The buildings stood on the west side of St. Anthony's Lane and their land stretched towards Henderson Street and the Yard heads. After the Reformation they were allowed to fall into ruin.

The Kings Wark was built in 1434 as a residence, storehouse and armoury for King James I. Invaders destroyed it in the early 16th century. It was a plague hospital in 1575, a tavern by 1613 (belonging to Bernard Lindsay who gave his name to Bernard Street), and a weigh house by 1690. After being destroyed again by fire it was from 1799 to 1822 a continental merchants and by 1959 a wine merchants, before returning to its present purpose as a pub.

The first bridge at Leith was built by Holyrood Abbey sometime between 1398 and 1439. It had three spans and wasn't demolished until the late 1700s.

Outbreaks and epidemics of disease were common in the early 15th Century, including dysentery, influenza, cholera, smallpox, measles typhus, TB, diphtheria and plague.

Chapter 4

The Burgh

The Shore, Leith – 10th June 1483

There she was, Alice Penderleith, coming out of Broad Wynd with her father. John Preston's heart missed a beat. She dazzled even from this distance.

He sat at a table outside Mrs McCafferty's tavern. The port's only respectable establishment, it was where most of the merchants and Burgesses met and deals were done. John turned his attention back to grumpy old Burgess Thompson, who sat across the table wrapped in a heavy cloak despite the warmth.

John needed to concentrate, difficult given that today was the day he was going to make a move. He had set eyes on her two years ago at this very spot. It had been love at first sight.

"The cloth, the fur and a barrel of wine for four bales of wool," said the grizzled Burgess.

"And eight silver pennies," said John.

Thompson looked him hard in the eye.

"Six silver pennies."

"Done," said John, holding out his hand.

Thompson gave a thin smile; they shook and marked the parchment.

Thompson rose. "Good to do business with you, Preston."

John nodded and smiled.

He left the tavern and moved into position on the quayside. He tried to look thoughtful, pretending to inspect a batch of cloth lying on top of a loaded cart. John's pulse quickened. He watched her closely as she strolled along the cobbles. She and her father knew the importance of first impressions, a contrast with the scruffily dressed porters, sailors, and carters unloading barrels of wine from a big Dutch Carrack onto wagons. John stood aside as the first of these trundled off towards the vaults at St Leonards Lands up near the Preceptory.

It had a muggy feel today; the sun had broken through; didn't look like there would be a shower after all. The air heavy with the scent of exotic spices from another ship, a Hulk from Bruges. On the quayside the usual arguments as the tacksmen argued with the skippers over the customs payments due to the Burgh. In the market at the bottom of the High Street everything was available from the stalls and booths. Fish and apples, ship's tackle and strong-smelling barrels of tar. The usual din of metal on wood and the smell of fresh hewn timber as the coopers kept up with the constant demand for barrels of whole, half and quarter sizes. More shouts and hammering from Cornton's boat yard a little further up river as carpenters, wrights, sawyers and sailmakers worked on a sleek looking new Galley.

Alice, beautiful as always, wore a white corseted gown over a blue striped petticoat, on her shoulders a red cloak of the best wool with a fur collar. A headdress with a peak framed the fine features of her oval face. Her eyes bright, her pale skin milky white. Her father's attire also paraded their wealth; a green doublet, open, showing off his expensive silk shirt. Hose tied at the waist with laces and wide toed leather shoes. His flat hat had a jewelled rim, dominated by a large sapphire centrepiece which sparkled in the sunlight. The pair brought a welcome dash of colour amid the shabby wooden houses, warehouses and booths that fronted the quay.

John moved into their path to intercept them. Then his muscles tensed, his brow furrowed as his mouth turned grim. To his dismay, climbing up the quayside ladder right beside him from a small rowboat below was the last person in the world he wanted to see, Rodger Hughes. John could sense his composure slipping away. Hughes's beefy figure reached the top of the ladder, dressed in an expensive looking deep purple cloak and silk shirt with puffed sleeves.

"Hughes," said John.

"Preston," Hughes nodded.

Then they just stared, grudgingly and wordlessly appraising each other.

John turned quickly to be the first to shake Alice's father's bony hand as they approached. Everything about the man was skinny, from his long face and nose down to his feet.

"Sir."

"Oh, ah yes ... eh... Preston."

Johns eyes narrowed; he forced a smile. Had he detected an evasive note in the voice? Something in the man's body language? He gave a small bow. John had worked hard to develop a familiarity with Alice's father over many months. He believed he'd achieved this through their various business dealings. *Was that an embarrassed expression on his face?* John sensed something had changed, but what?

"And Alice, how happy I am to see you." John gave her his widest grin.

With a special effort today, he was dressed in his finest cream linen tunic, a good fit on his lean frame – even combed his shaggy fair hair and washed his florid face. Alice acknowledged him with a nervous smile, lowered her beautiful eyes and then looked away. John's heart sank. Then, to John's horror, Alice's father greeted Hughes with a friendly smile; they exchanged whispered words and then he patted him on the back. John reeled, working hard to stop a frown forming.

He and Hughes had never seen eye to eye. They had fought on the very first day they met as children and although the smaller, John had given him a bloody nose. From that moment on the animosity between them had grown. Hughes was still bigger, but John always reckoned he could take him if necessary.

John had inherited his business from his father William, who had been great friends and partners with Hughes's father. Together they became successful merchants dealing in imports and exports. They had a mutually beneficial arrangement using John's father's Leith shipping connections and Hughes's father's contacts as a member of the all-powerful Edinburgh Burgesses.

When their fathers died, the two sons quickly split the business and soon developed a fierce rivalry. This animosity had only grown when John realised that Hughes also had designs on Alice. Her father stopped to take in the harbour scene.

"Looks like the rain will stay off, lovely," he said brushing a speck from his doublet. He pointed to the ship berthed on the opposite side. A group of carpenters were at work as it underwent repairs next to Thomas Diases boat yard.

"Look at the lines on that nice big Caravel; you're starting to see more of these in northern waters."

It had caused a stir when it arrived a few days earlier.

"Beautifully made, with its unusual shape and triangular lateen sail."

He turned to Hughes. "Maybe we should think of extending our investments to one of them."

Hughes gave a fawning smile.

"Well, we must get on," said her father turning to John. "Lots to do."

He walked on. John's colour rose. Alice smiled again but said nothing as she followed. Hughes's smirk turned into a sneer as he brushed past.

"You lose," he whispered.

Stunned, John watched them walk away. Something had gone very wrong.

It was only just after midday as John lifted the already half empty third tankard to his lips. He had gone to Leith's least salubrious tavern, the Pig and Bell in Rotten Row, known locally as the Stinking Pig because of the cesspit and a huge midden that sat next to it. Despite a strong odour the premises were busy, but he sat alone.

John was deflated. This morning was one of the worst of his life. He had been working on her father for two years and had now gone over it a hundred times trying to work out what had happened. They had even shaken on a verbal agreement a week or so before; a mutual business arrangement to share the let of one of the warehouses on the Shore.

The moment John set eyes on Alice it had been love at first sight, no doubt in his mind. He shivered at the memory. She was the only girl for him.

Most of his waking hours since had been focused on winning her hand. That she was the daughter of an Edinburgh Burgess would normally have been an insurmountable barrier for a Leith man, but John had believed that she could be his.

He realised what he had to do was climb the social ladder, and over the past couple of years he had managed to do just that, making his way up as a small scale but successful merchant, using his connections with Leith skippers. A few more years and he would have saved enough to buy into the Burgh. To become an Edinburgh Burgess, along with the rights and advantages that came with it. And if he married his way in, all the better. Even although that meant he had to leave Leith and move to live in Edinburgh, it would be well worth it for the hand of Alice Penderleith.

Today had been the day he would make his move; this morning he had planned to ask her father for her hand. He just couldn't fathom what had gone so wrong.

John finished his third and was considering whether to have a fourth tankard when a sudden commotion broke out on the other side of the room.

"Never."

Big Tam the carter smashed his fist down hard, causing the ale from several mugs to splatter across the table.

"Never in a million years," he bellowed, his great bulk looming over the others.

"I'm telling you Tam, that's what they are saying," replied the wizened little man beside him.

Tam's red face flushed.

"Willie, do you mean to tell me these bastards up in Edinburgh say that we Leith men don't have the right to trade at all, not with anyone?" he looked incredulous.

"That's what I heard," said wee Willie, his shrew-like face smug with a look of someone in the know. "I'm told that the Edinburgh Burgh has decided that their Burgesses may not go into any kind of partnership with a Leith man and that no Leith man can be involved in collecting the customs money due to the Burgh."

He paused and took a swig of his ale.

"What's more, I've also been informed that the Water Baillie's coming to tell us everything about it later today."

The crowded tavern was in uproar at the news as the implications began to sink in. John continued to sit in his corner seat. He stared over at the carters, white-faced. His gut wrenched as different scenarios flitted across his mind. His future success depended on him being able to continue to trade; he had lots of good contacts, far more than Hughes. The realisation started to hit home; this might be worse than just losing Alice.

It was now obvious that her father had seen this coming. John's business would be in trouble. For foreign trade, the power of the Royal Burgh of Edinburgh was total – he could not challenge their monopoly.

John sensed his world collapsing as it dawned on him that his arch rival in both business and love was going to gain an unassailable upper hand. Hughes lived in Edinburgh and had inherited a burgesship from his father. John was going to have to play second fiddle. The worst part was that he couldn't think what he might do about it. He lowered his head and held it in his hands as the reality hit him: this could be the end of all his hopes and dreams.

The grumbling in the tavern continued, and the news spread like wildfire. Soon the whole village was awash with rumour and counter-rumour. When the Baillie arrived, John joined the other men as they spilled out of the ale house; others gathered until most of the village's population was at the Shore.

The Water Baillie was Oswald Gilmoreson, an angry little man with bad skin, famed for his terrible breath. He had rheumy eyes, a pock marked face and a fat nose for such a thin man. Dressed in a top-quality black doublet and cloak he had the good sense to arrive with six men at arms bearing halberds and pikes. They helped him raise his wizened frame onto a barrel above the crowd.

He looked with scorn at the throng. Although he would never admit it and often complained about the difficulties he faced in the role of Water Baillie, everyone knew that in reality he enjoyed the power it gave him.

"Now, ladies and gentlemen," he said with an arrogant smirk, waving his hands to quieten them, "you all understand how it works."

He cleared this throat. "Unlike Leith, Edinburgh is a Royal Burgh, which has a number of rights granted by our beloved King."

He looked for a reaction but saw none.

"Only we who are Burgesses of the Burgh have the rights to trade with foreign countries. All shipped trade must go through us, and only us."

He stared into the eyes of everyone in the crowd.

"That's the law, and it's a law that unfortunately some of you have been breaking."

"Aye, your law," shouted big Tam the carter, "to fleece us and to feather your own nest with our hard work."

The Baillie looked flustered, then he composed himself and stuck out his chest and stood as tall as his crooked frame allowed.

"The harbour," he said spreading his hands, "and everything that comes and goes from it belongs to Edinburgh," he paused for effect, pointing at the mob, "not to you."

Within seconds a murmur rose among the Leithers; it quickly became shouts. Two young men surged forward angrily and the men at arms barred the way. A scuffle broke out and despite the Water Baillie's attempts to calm the throng, the meeting dissolved into chaos, forcing the soldiers to raise and swing their weapons. The angry crowd continued to press forward as the Baillie clambered down among the melee and made a hasty retreat. He climbed on his horse and galloped off towards the eastern road out of the port, having made the wise decision that with the locals in this mood he was quite likely to get lynched.

The crowd dispersed, but resentment remained, and would linger and grow. John returned to the Pig and Bell. He sensed a rage developing in his gut. He realised he was powerless –what could one man do against the authority of the Burgesses of Edinburgh? That evening as darkness fell, he came to the river with his tools. By the light of the moon he worked late into the night.

*

The next morning John watched from his vantage point on the Shore. At first, he felt a stab of jealousy on seeing them as they arrived from Edinburgh soon after dawn, Hughes and Alice arm in arm, accompanied by her father. Being a Sunday, John's plan depended on her father following his usual routine. They left their horses at the stable in Cables Wynd and strolled across the bridge to visit his business interests on the north side of the river.

They made their way to various premises: a fish dryer, a builder of small fishing boats and a blacksmith's shop. When they turned east along Hie Gait, John knew his plan had worked. They were heading to church; their destination the new South Leith Chapel, and John now knew how they would get there. Rather than double back over the bridge they headed towards the river mouth. Then down to the beach at the water's edge to the rowing boat her father kept there.

They were smiling as Hughes pushed the boat from the bank and they climbed aboard, Alice prim alongside her father at the back while Hughes took the oars. John could hardly contain himself as they set off and were soon halfway across. Both Alice and her father laughed out loud at something that Hughes said.

A thin smile crossed John's lips as he watched the expressions on the faces of Alice and her father as they realised what was happening. The boat began to list, fear etched on her father's wizened features. Alice screamed. The boat then seemed to disintegrate as the clinker planks started to come apart. Two nearby swans flapped their wings, disturbed by the commotion.

The boat started to sink. Panic set in. Alice struggled with her beautiful dress as it billowed around her, her hands grasping for Hughes and he, panic on his face, forcefully pushing her away and scrabbling for an oar, which was the only thing still floating. Her father was floundering, shouting and splashing in terror. By the time people on the bank began to organise a rescue craft, John's smile widened. His heart had broken and may never recover but there was a wicked satisfaction in this small revenge. John turned and walked back up the Shore towards his home at Rotten Row. His smile vanished; the sadness seemed to grow. He knew now that it may overwhelm him.

At one of the food stalls he saw old Burgess Thompson accompanied by his even older looking wife. John nodded in acknowledgement.

"Ah, Preston, hello again."

John stopped dead. A sudden rush of adrenaline coursed through him. He trembled, as if hit by a bolt of lightning.

"Eh … a… I…" he stuttered, unable to find the right words.

From behind the old couple had stepped a ray of sunlight in a blue dress. John felt almost as if he had a physical pain in his heart. He rubbed his eyes and looked again.

"You have met my wife, and this is my granddaughter, Annabel," said Thompson.

Annabel smiled a coy smile. She simply took his breath away. Where had the old man been hiding her all this time? She was surely the most beautiful girl he had ever seen in his life.

There was absolutely no doubt in his mind.

It was love at first sight.

Historical Note

South Leith Parish Church was first built as a chapel in 1483. The present building dates from 1847.

The Edinburgh Burgesses would elect from their number a "Water Baillie" who would govern Leith affairs which affected Edinburgh's trade.

Over the centuries Edinburgh Burgesses passed several pieces of legislation to protect their own interests and curb Leith residents' opportunities to trade.

The High Street is now known as Tolbooth Wynd.

Rotten Row was developed into Water Street.

After 800 years Hie Gait was renamed Sandport Street in the 19th century. It was the original high-water mark of the river. The river narrowed significantly as North Leith developed southwards.

Chapter 5

The Ships

Hie Gait, North Leith – 10th July 1513

"They want me there – why?" Thomas Preston's large brown eyes widened, fearful at the prospect.

"The King's cousin the Earl of Arran, for goodness' sake; what would high and mighty people like him want with the likes of me? I'm just a cart driver."

His next-door neighbour McGilvery's weather-beaten face creased into a smile. "Get your cloak, I'll wait for you," he said as Thomas turned back into the narrow little wooden house, crammed amongst the others on Hie Gait.

Jean lay on the bed. Thomas couldn't help but look at her curves under the thin woollen blanket. She fiddled with her nails. A sweet smile on her rosebud lips.

"What did Captain McGilvery want?"

"I've to go to a secret meeting," whispered Thomas. He was thin and rangy, fair hair, long, sideburns, a worried expression on his sharp features.

"A secret meeting about what?"

He shrugged. Jean grabbed his shirtsleeve as he reached across for his cloak and pulled him onto her. She hugged him; Thomas could feel her body, lithe as a cat, pressed hard against his. Thomas sighed long and hard.

She looked up from beneath her smoky eyelashes. Thomas knew she sensed his discontentment. He pulled away.

"I've not got time for this," his voice cold.

"I've been honest with you right from the beginning. Let's keep it simple, I said when you first took me to your bed." Jean's eyes flashed, angry, and wounded. Thomas turned away, grabbed his cloak, and stomped out the door.

McGilvery led Thomas along Hie Gait, past St Ninian's Chapel and across the bridge. They made their way along the Shore towards the river's mouth.

Was it time to call things off? No hard feelings? She would be much to give up…

Jean had appeared content with their arrangement at first. She now seemed less so. He didn't want any of that marriage stuff. She had hinted a few weeks before but given his unenthusiastic reaction, she hadn't pushed it.

Jean was a lovely girl and doing very well for one so young with so many sailors in the port. Despite her youth she now ran three girls from her place in Rotten Row. When Thomas had first met her, she had been a working girl herself but she now assured him he was the only one sharing her bed. He believed her. He was in turmoil, what to do?

The harbour was jammed. Ships laid four abreast along the wharf creaked and tugged at their moorings. The fast-flowing river high after yesterday's heavy rain showers. Seagulls wheeled and squawked below a thin grey cloud. Two swans flapped their wings. The warm air pungent with the smell of rotting fish, sawn timber and seaweed.

A three-masted carrack, one hundred and fifty feet long and low-built turned clumsily at the harbour mouth. On deck the crew struggled to reposition a twelve-pound cannon. Others ran up the rigging or worked on the windlass. There was the squeal of halliards running through blocks as her topsails loosened. Elsewhere big Galleys and Carracks fought for space with smaller single sail Picards. Sails were dressed, chains rattled, barrels of provisions rolled and stacked. Hulls pulled on their cables and ropes were coiled; a buzz of activity wherever you looked.

If Jean's looking for someone permanent or predictable, he's not for her. Didn't she understand the work of a carter was erratic? He had to take any job whenever it came. He was getting plenty of work over the last month or two due to the activity surrounding the fleet, but no guarantee it would last. He'd never be the rich man she wanted.

The King's fleet was preparing for war; the word was that fifteen great ships would sail soon to help the French in the conflict with the English.

A hammering and shouts came from the boat repair yards. They were working at full stretch. The taverns were full, mariners had come from many other parts of Scotland to join with their French allies. Thomas had no memory of the village ever having been so busy. The brewers struggled to keep up with the demand for ale. Jean had told him that all the brothels were so busy the working girls spent little time on their feet.

Everywhere was crowded: the houses, stables and cellars all along the Shore. Stalls supplemented the usual shops and booths with the increase in demand. Everything was available. Blocks of salt, vegetables, chickens in wooden cages, farm tools and lethal-looking weapons. A stink came from the butcher's stall, pig's heads, offal and black puddings.

McGilvery pointed. "*The Great Michael.*"

Thomas looked seaward beyond the sandbar at the harbour's entrance. He at once sensed a wave of pride course through him. Sitting outside the harbour mouth by the Black Rocks lay Scotland's greatest ever ship, *The Great Michael*, the biggest ship in the world. Its four massive oak masts and drooping giant sails sat comfortably in the light swell. Even as a lowly carter he had played his part in its construction along with many other residents of Leith. It had taken eight years to build and only been completed the year before along at Newhaven Dock. Thomas had made his contribution with hundreds of other rope-makers, shipwrights, sawyers, nail and sail-makers. Now it would soon be on its way with the others to fight alongside the French against King Henry the VIII's fleet.

The light started to fade. The new fire beacons at the harbour mouth had been lit and would soon cast a weak light across the Shore's cobbles. McGilvery and Thomas moved into the shadows and tried to make themselves inconspicuous as they neared the meeting place.

They arrived at the Kings Wark, the King's storehouse workshops and armoury. Thomas and McGilvery were led to a basement. It was dark, a scent of tallow from candles that lit the gloom. They were the last to arrive. The Earl of Arran, the fleet commander sat at the head of the table. He wore an expensive-looking light-coloured sleeveless leather jerkin over a green silk doublet. His black hair swept back, touched with a hint of grey, his beard clipped. The rest of the table occupied by Leith skippers. With McGilvery's arrival, there was now a total of nine.

"Gentlemen," said Arran. The large sapphire broach pinned to his chest sparkled in the candlelight; it dazzled.

These men each skippered a ship of the Scots fleet. Thomas was aware that they formed a group of a new class of mariner. As an unfree port under Edinburgh's control, the local merchants had limited opportunities. Thomas knew this well; his own father had a merchant business in Leith that failed years ago, turned him to drink and an early grave. Yet these were men who, despite the best efforts of Edinburgh brought a new wealth to Leith with their skill, daring and enterprise. Thomas took a seat, a tankard of ale placed in front of him.

"Our spies in London have told us we have a problem." Arran paused to caress his luxurious moustache. "It appears we have a saboteur in our midst."

There was a low murmur around the room.

"And if we don't find him our whole scheme might be at risk."

The murmur got louder. Arran waited.

"Our informers have told us it's likely to be a senior figure on one of the ships of the fleet."

"But how can we find out who?" said the gruff-looking captain next to Thomas. Only his keen eyes showed among his thick beard and moustache. "It might be anyone and the town is jam-packed; it will be as hard as finding a pebble on the beach."

"It will be difficult," said Arran, "but not impossible."

He stopped and drank from his wine cup.

"We can narrow the options. In my heart I'm certain it's not going to be one of you Leith men – you would never betray us."

All the men nodded in approval; they had all known each other all their lives, their bond was strong.

"What that means is we need to concentrate on the six French ships in our fleet. There's got to be a connection. The only question is, what?"

A murmur broke out again.

"Do we have any further information?" said McGilvery.

Lord Arran looked contemplative for a moment.

"What we have discovered is that the English ambassador, a Dr West, is in the area along with his entourage. The official line is that he is here to discuss diplomatic relations, but it's clear that he has been watching our preparations and he will feed that information back to London."

Arran stood up, moved to the barrel of wine by the wall, and refilled his goblet.

"My view is that there has to be some connection between the ambassador, and the saboteur – if we can find that then we may be able to act."

Thomas had been following the conversation with interest. There was a gap in the discussion.

"Eh," he said and raised his hand. "What am I doing here?"

Arran made a slow turn and looked straight at him with sharp hazel eyes. Thomas's hands trembled.

"Ah, Mr Preston," said Arran.

Thomas looked confused.

"You may have a very important part to play. You have come with the high recommendation of your good neighbour here," he said nodding towards McGilvery. "I'm told that you have a personal acquaintance with every thief, vagabond, pickpocket and whore in the port of Leith."

Thomas looked surprised for a moment, but then nodded. Arran moved back to the table and took his seat.

"Well, then you can help us. The ambassador's entourage comprises only three senior men; we are working to the theory that it's one of them."

Thomas nodded slowly.

"What we need is to watch them and to follow them discreetly. I need to discover if there's a connection between them and any of the French ship's officers."

Arran took out a leather purse and threw it across the table, where it landed with the clink of coin. Thomas picked it up. It was heavy.

"Do you think you could arrange that?"

Thomas laughed nervously, but then realised the idea appealed to him. His job with his cart took him all around town every day. He was on personal terms with every resident of Leith, be they high or low born. Plus, he loved to gossip. If there was anything to know about anyone. Thomas knew it. He was a goldmine of local information. Thomas had always been interested in everyone else's business. His mother had often told him he was nosy.

Thomas hesitated for a moment, then nodded. "Yes, that's something I can organise."

*

Thomas went to work at once. By the time he returned to his house in the Hie Gait later that night he had handpicked and briefed the necessary collection of people. Jean could also have a crucial part to play. She was in a foul mood following their earlier exchange. But once he had explained the situation along with what it required, she quickly agreed. That night they made love, their earlier friction forgotten.

The next morning Thomas felt jumpy as he carried out his usual tasks supplying victuals to the ships. He sweated, not just from the effort of loading the supplies onto his cart at the warehouse. *Had he chosen the right people to help?* A whore, a con man, a gambler and two pickpockets. All of whom he would trust with his life. On the wagon he piled a pound of biscuit, pork, and salt beef. A quarter pound of butter, a half of cheese and a gallon of beer for each and every man on board before delivering it to a ship.

Then later with a load of salt fish, flour, oatmeal and eggs he met as arranged with his spies. No developments. He reminded them of the need for the greatest discretion as they tracked the English diplomats.

The day wore on. Thomas felt on edge. There was no new information. He experienced a growing frustration with the lack of any breakthrough, and by the evening he was losing hope. Time was running out.

*

Jean sat in her usual place at the front door of her establishment in Rotten Row. The warm air heavy with the smell of perfume. It was one of the town's more upmarket brothels. Wealthier clients frequented. As well as having the best girls she always made an effort to keep the rooms looking nice and even changed the sheets from time to time. Her eyebrows narrowed as the connection clicked in her mind. Had she detected a sleight of hand out of the corner of her eye? The Frenchman had been leaving as the Englishman arrived and she was aware that he was the Ambassador's clerk.

Had something passed between them? She waited until the clerk was occupied with one of the girls. She stood outside the door until she heard grunts of ecstasy and then made her move. She crawled into the room then rummaged in the pile of clothes left on the floor at the end of the bed. In one pocket, she found it. A small piece of parchment. She recognised the seal at once. She had struck gold.

She crawled back out quietly and left the house. A dash back along the Shore and over the bridge and onto Thomas's in Hie Gait. Thomas was outside and attending to the harness on his horse. He looked pensive.

He looked up. "Anything?"

Jean kept her face straight.

"What would it be worth… If I found something?"

Thomas raised his eyebrows.

"Name your price."

"Then I think I may have what you are looking for." With a casual smile she slipped the paper out of her pocket and held it up tantalisingly. Thomas couldn't contain his excitement when he saw the seal.

"Oh, you little gem, Jean, you don't know how much this might mean." He planted a kiss on her forehead then danced a little jig of joy.

"Give it here, I must see Lord Arran."

As he reached for the parchment Jean pulled it away and pushed it deep between her breasts. She shook her head. Thomas looked puzzled.

"Now, Thomas," she said, "let's talk about our future."

Historical Note

The Great Michael was soon sold to the French, rarely used and left to rot.

King James IV's fleet was built up over a ten-year period and soon sailed to support the French against the English. But a storm had split up the French fleet and the English escaped. The Scots skippers then had to dash home when news reached them of a terrible defeat at the battle of Flodden. This defeat had severe repercussions for the country. It lost its King and much of its nobility. There followed many years of political instability in Scotland.

Chapter 6

The Invaders

The Shore, Leith – 3rd May 1544

Catherine Preston cleaned it carefully with a rag. She noticed her hands trembling. She secreted it among her skirts wrapped in a piece of linen, threw the rag in the fire and left the room on the top floor and came down the stairs.

In the distance, cannon fire. She peered through the small panes of lead strip window that overlooked the harbour. There was panic on the waterfront. Shopkeepers and residents piling their valuables into any available transport; carts of all sizes, packhorses, a wheelbarrow and even on their own back. The wet cobbles already strewn with things discarded in haste; a broken chair, an enormous cooking pot, a shoe and what looked an old pair of hose. In the harbour, a handful of sailors on the deck of the ship, trying to salvage objects of value that could be carried away overland.

Far outside the river mouth, Catherine saw the English ships gliding up the grey firth. Surprised how beautiful they looked moving in a line with full sail on a stiff easterly breeze. The rumour that thousands of invading troops were landing up towards Newhaven.

She spent a few minutes checking her clothes with care. She yanked up her woollen tunic and checked the linen smock underneath. *Were there any stains?* She was relieved to discover none. She took off her bonnet and pulled down her long, fair hair; she scraped her hands over her head and shook it before replacing her cap.

She heard a kerfuffle on the landing; everything of value was being taken downstairs. All the tavern staff rushing around carrying what they could.

"Help me with these drapes, girl," shouted Mrs Buchan from the stairway, her manner sharp as always. Catherine made a final check of her clothes before going to help her pull them off the wall. A cloud of dust billowed as they came crashing to the floor. Catherine folded them together.

Then a call from downstairs, Mr Buchan's loud gravel voice, coloured with a hint of desperation. "We need to go and we need to go right now – and I mean now."

She saw fear etched on his wife's face, as she ran downstairs with the drapes. Mr Charles Buchan stood in the centre of the tavern's hallway gesticulating and shouting orders. Dressed with care as always, in a close-fitting red doublet, a colour that matched his flustered face. Slender despite his middle age, with a fine chiselled nose and weak chin – but there was dread in his eyes. The cooks, maids and stable boys were carrying everything out the door and piling it into the wagon. The horse stood snorting and stomping in a thin drizzle.

She considered telling Mr Buchan what happened, stared at him hoping he would see. That he somehow understood. *If the panic stopped, they might be able to go over it. To comprehend.* She pushed the thought away it was stupid; she understood how harassed he was, trying to save his livelihood, all their livelihoods, and what difference would it make, what could he do? She needed to cope with this on her own.

She stepped out the door, the smell of seaweed, old fish and damp in the salt air hit her, as she added the drapes to the increasing pile in the cart.

On the quayside two ships swung on their moorings, one of them huge. The King's flagship *The Salamander* with its row of big guns protruding from its side. It appeared abandoned. A mess of ropes and sails lay unattended in a heap on the deck. The last sailors were leaving and stumbling over the debris of fish entrails, nets and pots that littered the quay, one carrying a barrel and the other struggling with a large ship's bell.

At the tavern entrance two young officers in short sleeved leather jerkins struggled to fit into their breastplates. They looked tense. One of them smiled, Peter, the youngest one. Tall and handsome. Catherine liked Peter; she forced her sweet face into a smile in return.

"Have you informed the captain?" said the other brusquely.

"Yes sir," said Catherine with a small curtsy

"The captain said to tell you he will follow on."

Peter turned and approached her. She thought he was going to say something. *Could she tell him?*

"Quick, quick, everyone," shouted Mr Buchan bursting out the door with a large vase in his hands. He thrust it at Catherine. She turned away, the moment with Peter gone. The two officers then joined the small group of troops waiting in line on the Shore. They looked nervous; Catherine watched as they marched off with the clank of metal on metal. Among them her younger brother Fergus, just a boy; she had not even had time to say goodbye. Most carried long pikes, a few with a double-edged Leith axe on their shoulder. One staggered under the weight of a heavy gun, an arquebus musket. *Surely there were far too few of them to offer much resistance?*

Catherine hoisted the vase onto the cart. The others added more chairs, stools, drapes, tankards for ale, and food, the wagon now overflowing,

"We can take no more," shouted Mrs Buchan.

Catherine had been working in the Buchan's tavern for the past two years. It could have been worse. They were kind enough, although they always kept them busy. Catherine would rise before dawn for long hours of washing, clearing, tidying, fetching and serving. But it hadn't been all work; they enjoyed themselves sometimes. The most important thing was that the little money she made helped keep her mother and her going. With Mother too ill to serve now, Catherine's wage was their only income to pay the rent on their tiny bare room around the corner in Water Street. Catherine was glad her mother had left with little Michael a few days before, when rumours of the invasion increased, and gone to her cousin up in Edinburgh.

The two junior officers had billeted with them for the last month along with their senior, the Captain. The town had been preparing for weeks for some kind of trouble. Catherine knew the defences had been improved – it was very relaxed, nobody believed anything would happen. It was obvious now that such complacency had been misplaced. She saw it with her own eyes; the English were invading.

Catherine grimaced as a flash of memory from the day before flitted across her mind. She had been setting the fire in the Captain's room. Catherine remembered the steps outside, the thump of big boots on the wooden floor. A shudder of disgust coursed through her at the thought. She knew it was him even before he entered; she would recognise that slow, heavy step anywhere.

During the first few weeks the banter had been fun. She liked young Peter; such a nice smile and she went out of her way to offer the soldiers the best of service, making sure their tankards were filled and serving their food when off duty.

Then she became aware of the Captain taking an interest, knew by the way he looked at her. Sensed his eyes following her every time she passed. She began to wish she hadn't been so pretty. She'd thought nothing of it in the beginning, no different from plenty of other men. Smile and turn away, that usually worked.

Then he started to become bolder. The way he deliberately brushed against her. Laughing when she passed, and he had made an aside to the others. Then once he'd groped her when drunk. It stopped being so much fun. It had started to feel uncomfortable.

She felt her skin crawl as she remembered his words in his room.

"And how is my young filly today?" he'd said as he walked towards her. His smile had turned into a leer. She could smell the spirit on his breath. She said nothing and looked away, had learned that with him that was the best way. She had sought to move past, but she was penned in. He laughed; she had no retreat. He was big and fat, with a slobbery mouth, but strong. He looked like a pig, and a dog, and she soon discovered he had an appetite like both. He had put his hand on her breast; she had struggled to move but he grasped it tight.

"I've been watching you, my dear, I've seen the way you look at young Peter. Like him, do you?"

Catherine remembered realising she was frozen to the spot; she failed to make her legs work.

"Time for a real man, my beauty."

Then it happened, all the hurt and the pain, the humiliation. The worst part was serving him a meal afterwards pretending everything was normal. It only crossed her mind later that she should have poisoned it, but she had still been in shock.

"Right everybody," called Mr Buchan as he climbed into the driver's seat of the cart. "Time to leave, lets stick together, we will probably return in a few days and everyone can go back to normal." He crossed himself. "The Lord will protect us."

With a shake of the reins the horse took the strain, and they rumbled off towards the eastern road out of the port, Mr Buchan and his wife in the cart and the rest pushing on foot.

They joined the others heading out of town. After a hundred yards the trickle turned into a throng. There was soon a long line of carts; others carried what they could in wheelbarrows or on their shoulders. Possessions of all kinds along with screaming children. The recent torrential rain had made the path a mire. It was heavy going. Several old and infirm had already fallen by the wayside unable to move further. In the distance they heard cannon fire and shouts coming from the direction of Newhaven. Panic increased as some tried to quicken their pace. The sounds, yells and cannon shot and the clash of metal seemed closer.

A small group of Cavalry came down the road from Edinburgh towards the battle. There was a crush, one cart turned over, several were injured, there were screams of terror. Catherine shuddered. *What if she was pregnant?*

Then a horseman came charging along the Newhaven road with blood on his shirt. "They have landed!" he screamed. "There are thousands of them."

They got the wagon as far as the bottom of the eastern road. It became stuck in a boggy section. Together with a great effort they worked to free it.

"We must make it lighter," screamed Mr Buchan as he threw the vase Catherine had carried onto the ground with a smash. Furniture followed. After a struggle they managed to get it out of the mire and staggered on with the rest of the throng. Catherine realised she was trembling. The path was thick mud with so many people. She trudged on, putting one foot in front of the other. *If she was pregnant, what would she do?*

It was slow progress. They made it to the top of the eastern road when disaster struck. A sudden loud crack as the axle snapped. The light was fading. It was turning colder. Catherine saw Mr Buchan's shoulders slump, his fine red doublet now covered in mud. There was nothing to be done. He made the decision.

"Abandon the cart, we can continue on foot."

Catherine glanced back over the line of people making their way up the slope. The first signs of smoke rising back in the town. *If pregnant, could she keep it? Or would she get rid of it? Was she capable of committing murder and killing it?*

They had nearly reached the top of the Abbey Hill as darkness started to fall.

Who would have believed it? Only yesterday it would have been unthinkable. A murderer in the family. Her mother had once run a brothel, but a murderer, what would she and her brother say? Then she recalled her mother once telling her a family story of a distant relation from a long, long time ago. He'd murdered a priest in Leith and had to run away. That's what she would do – she would run.

Catherine decided that she would keep walking. See her mother and wee Michael and then keep going. Go west, Glasgow maybe, or even Ireland. She would leave them if necessary. *And what about Fergus, her brother, was he even still alive?*

It was dark by the time they reached the crest of the Abbey Hill. They all turned and peered back. A bright glow lit the sky. There were flames, the whole of Leith burning. In the gloom Catherine saw the sorrow etched on Mr Buchan's face as he realised his tavern would never escape such a fire. Catherine fingered the object wrapped in her skirts. The knife taken from the kitchen at dawn. He was snoring when she had gone to his room that morning.

"The invaders have come," said Mr Buchan, sadness in his voice.

She remembered the brief resistance from the eyeball before it pierced through. Then it had gone in easily, very deep. Blood. His other eye shot open, and she had watched his flabby mouth twitching.

Agape with a silent scream.

"Yes" she replied softly. "The invaders."

Historical Note

The Earl of Hertford's invasion of Edinburgh and burning of Leith in 1544 was part of the "Rough wooing", a war between England and Scotland which broke out when King Henry VIII tried to force a marriage alliance between the two-year-old Mary Queen of Scots and his son and heir Prince Edward and also to destroy the "auld alliance" between Scotland and France.

Chapter 7

The Siege

Pelham Mount, Leith Links – 22nd April 1560

"**B**ugger this," gasped Michael, "I'm running tonight."

Big Fergus Preston was on his knees. Thick cloying mud covered his breeches and jacket. His long fair hair dripping onto his pointed stubbled jaw. Exhausted after carrying so many heavy cannonballs over the fifty yards of sodden rough ground. He sat panting heavily. His younger brother Michael dropped down beside him. Fergus grabbed him by the lapel and yanked his scrawny frame towards him until their faces were almost touching.

"Don't be so stupid, you wouldn't stand a chance."

The English artillerymen at the big gun looked at them with a quizzical glance. Fergus lowered his voice to a whisper, his sharp features now grim. "Look, I've already lost two of my best friends – I don't want to lose my wee brother as well," he hissed.

"You'll be hung after they have flogged you."

"Stuff you, Fergus," said Michael pushing him away. "We need to escape from here or we will die. If it's not by being blown up by the bloody French, it will be through overwork from that bastard Duncan."

The horse from the wagon that brought the balls up from the fleet's landing area at Portobello broke its leg and couldn't make the last yards up to Pelham's big cannon. Captain Duncan made it clear in his usual far from friendly way that they needed to be carried up by hand. The two spent most of the day transporting over sixty balls and at last they had built a neat triangular pile next to the big gun.

It had been a long day; the sun never broke through the heavy cloud, and a thin drizzle made the task even more difficult. The high defensive walls that protected Leith were only three hundred yards away through the gloom. Fergus and Michael crouched behind the wooden barricades protecting the great cannon. With it the Congregation Army had been bombarding the French positions in the port for the past ten days.

Michael grunted as together they lifted the last ball and put it on the top of the pile. The following day that ball would arc over the town's defences and land at the foot of Burgess Street, bounce on the flagstones on the Shore and shear the front legs off a horse before ending up in one of the large mooring rings by the river. The horse made a welcome addition to the diet of the besieged French.

"Shut it," snapped Fergus.

"If anyone hears you, Duncan will have you swinging, you know what he's like."

"We could get away and he would never catch us."

"Don't you believe it, and what if we win this battle, what then?" hissed Fergus, desperation in his voice. "Where could we hide? I want to return to Leith after this."

"Well stuff it, I'm going," said Michael, his voice trembling.

"Look don't be stupid – don't you want to get these Frenchies out of our town; is that not worth fighting for? I want revenge after what they did to our home, so you and I are staying until we do that."

Michael bared his teeth. "For god's sake don't you tell—"

Suddenly from behind the cannon appeared the looming shape of Captain "the preacher" Duncan. He strode up fast and punched Michael hard in the back of the head.

"Blasphemer!" he screamed with his finger an inch from Michaels face. "How dare you take the Lord's name in vain? You will know God's wrath."

The Captain was a great bear of a man, tall and broad with large whiskers and a deep scar on his left cheek. He wore a leather jerkin with his huge muscular arms bared. He stared at them with fierce, piercing eyes. Fergus and Michael knew it would be a brave man who stood up to him. Duncan only had two ways of behaving; either he snarled orders at the men or else he spouted religion, but with a snarl.

"Put on the armour of God so you can take a stand against the devils' schemes," he hissed.

Michael felt the spray of spittle on his face.

"Now get to work, you swabs or one of these popish Frenchie soldiers will be sticking a bayonet up your arse."

They said nothing but waited with bated breath. Every nerve was telling them to run from this madman but they knew it best to sit still and hope for the storm to pass. Fergus kept a firm grip on Michael's sleeve.

Duncan turned away. They looked at each other and together sighed in relief.

*

It was hard to believe it was only a week ago. Fergus knew it had changed Michael.

The French broke out and attacked at first light; a cavalry charge backed up by a thousand infantry. It was a tremendous shock; the last thing they were expecting. In their two years in the army it was the first time they had seen any real action; a terrifying experience. One minute Fergus, Michael and their two friends were building a fire to cook their breakfast next to the big gun's defensive wooden wall. The next thing they were running for their lives trying to escape French steel. They had been badly shaken, and such sadness; their two comrades dead.

It had been a disaster, over two hundred of the Congregation Army's men killed on and around the links. With no one to tell them what to do, they turned tail and ran for it; they lost their friends in the panic. To make matters worse, the next day Duncan made them return and help pick up and bury the dead. Michael had been the one to come across the mutilated bodies of their pals. He had gone into himself after that.

They were attached to the artillery unit that arrived with the English army, their job to support the big gun. Cleaning equipment, lifting and carrying and looking after the ammunition and horses. They spent many hours digging to create the defensive wall around the raised area that was now Pelham's defence.

Finding out what was happening was hard. The war always appeared to keep changing. A few months before, it looked grim. The French seemed to have the Protestant army on the run but then the English arrived with a large fleet, bringing reinforcements and guns.

Things swung back in their favour. Despite the success of their surprise attack they now pinned down 3,000 French troops with the siege of the town. The gun emplacements surrounding it had kept up a regular bombardment of the walls.

*

The sun at last broke through just as it started to set; the shadows lengthened until at last the order came to stand down. Together they moved back from the front line and towards the beach and hastily erected a camp. They salivated at the thought of a hot meal as they made their way through the myriad of carts, guns, men and horses that made up the siege army. As darkness fell, they along with around thirty of their unit of pike men, bowmen, porters and horse handlers sat around the fire. They huddled together and shivered as a thick haar moved in from the sea.

Fergus and Michael had joined up with the reformation army two years earlier. Before that Fergus had worked as a porter at the harbour. The French arrived in Leith six years before. Things seemed fine at first, the local Lords appeared happy with the arrangement. Then it started to turn sour. Despite food shortages the French always appeared to have enough. Then when their mother discovered that they wanted to commandeer all the houses in Water Street, that was the final straw; enough was enough.

He and Michael ran away to Edinburgh to join the army of the Lords of the Congregation who had set themselves up as a protestant anti-French force. The pair had been further inspired when they went to hear John Knox speak. They now knew their cause was just.

It was hard work but although he didn't like to admit it at first, Fergus had quite enjoyed it. Along with Michael and their pals they had great adventures as the war swung back and forward, up to Perth and Stirling. The food wasn't bad, and they became very fit. Leith had now changed all that. The devastating attack at Pelham Mount along with the madness of Captain Duncan altered their views.

They hunched around the fire. The squad were young men from all over Scotland with a smattering of seasoned campaigners. One of these was auld Jimmy, tough as old boots, but fair, and popular with the younger men. He was a Leith man who had fought alongside Fergus as a boy when Hertford invaded some years before, at the same time as Fergus's sister Catherine had vanished.

"The things you said last night, Jimmy, explain it again," said Michael.

"It's simple," said Jimmy, his wrinkled face staring into the thin vegetable broth he stirred in a big cauldron. "Nowadays good Leith men like yersel' are fighting alongside the English to get rid of the bastard French."

"Aye we know that."

"Aye, but aboot fifteen year ago it was a different world from what we have now." Jimmy raised an eyebrow. "Back then good Leithers like ourselves were fighting alongside the French to get rid of the bastard English after Lord Hertford razed the town."

"But how did that happen, what changed?"

"What's changed is that good Leithers like yersel' are now fighting with protestants against the papists."

"Aye."

"While back then good Leithers like yersel' were fighting alongside the papists against the protestants."

"But why?" said Michael. "It makes no sense."

"That's a good question," said Jimmy with a chuckle. "If a kent that I'd be a lord and not a horse handler."

After eating, Fergus wrapped himself in his blanket and huddled beside his brother.

"Remember when we were wee," whispered Michael. "I used to love the Catholic church. There was nothing else on in winter; the church was the best show in town, all that smoke and singing."

"So did I. Funny how things change. I remember that Mum would never have considered challenging the ways of the priests. These were men ordained by God – she couldn't imagine them ever being wrong."

"That was then, this is now," said Michael ruefully.

"Aye but I remember my old boss," said Fergus. "He was a timber merchant when I worked at the harbour and was always ranting on about how it was ridiculous that everything had to involve the church. He said the local bishop was a bandit who controlled all the commerce. They were corrupt and took bribes; he was desperate to see the church loses its power. That's why he became a protestant."

"Guess we joined the reformation army because the French wanted Mother's house," said Michael.

"To be honest, I don't understand that religious stuff. And when you listen to what auld Jimmy has to say, it's just confusing."

*

Next morning Captain Duncan's shouts woke Fergus as the sun rose. The rain had cleared, and it was bright.

"Come to the Lord, boys, come and hear the Lord's word," he shouted as he made his way through the group kicking them awake.

"Oh shit, it's Sunday," said Fergus as he turned to his brother.

His whole body jolted as he saw Michaels's bed empty, his bag gone.

Fergus stood up and looked around. *Oh no*, he thought in a panic. "Michael, you idiot," he whispered to himself.

Captain Duncan now pulled himself onto the back of an ammunition cart. He gave a fierce stare as the men ambled forward and gathered sleepily in front of it. Then, leaning forward he closed his eyes; he held the sides of the cart so hard his knuckles were white. He seemed to tremble. His face contorted, and he looked skywards, his expression full of fervent passion as he sought the words. The men stood, silent and sullen. The captain's dramatic silence stretched. He held his breath, then, "Papists!" he screamed, and he smashed his fist onto the side of the cart, the sound echoing around the group like a gunshot. With his other hand, he held his bible up to the heavens, pages flapping in the light wind, its spine broken from previous rough treatment.

"Papists!" he screamed again. "They have no right to call themselves the followers of Christ," he bellowed. "Papists, they are sinners, they are pollution on the land." He hammered home each word with an emotion that he hoped would become imprinted on the hearts of his men. "Priests are fornicators, they are corrupt."

Fergus's mind raced. He felt the tension in every muscle in his body.

Michael, oh Michael.

Duncan raged on and within minutes he reached the point where it didn't matter if he made sense, his sole aim to lash his men into a frenzy. They looked on with barely an expression.

"Papists and their devil in Rome will be doomed in the deepest pits of hell for all eternity." He waved his arms dramatically. "You must armour yourself with the shield of faith, men; we must whip them like dogs."

The first cannon fire of the day came from the French side as the sermon came to an end. Duncan gave the order to move back into the front line. As they packed up and prepared to move off, an English cavalry patrol came trotting into the camp. Fergus's heart sank.

The two cavalrymen were towing someone behind them like a dog on a leash. It was Michael, his hands tied. The patrol stopped in front of Captain Duncan. Michael fell to his knees.

Fergus shuddered, he felt faint.

"Wait," ordered Duncan.

Fergus could only watch in horror as Duncan ordered the setting up of a flogging post. He then pulled a horsewhip from the cart. He swung it above his head. The two patrolmen threw a rope with a noose over the bow of a tree.

Duncan screamed for the men to gather round to watch the punishment of the deserter. They tied Michael to the flogging post. The captain ripped off his shirt baring his back. His brother turned his head; his pleading eyes found Fergus.

Fergus could only turn and look away.

Historical Note

The defensive walls around Leith at this time were similar to those that can still be seen at Berwick upon Tweed. They were roughly in line with Constitution Street, Great Junction Street and Admiralty Street. No trace of them remains.

Traditionally it's believed that Giant's Brae on Leith Links is the site of Pelham's mount gun emplacement although there is some debate about this.

In 1558 a group of noblemen, styling themselves the Lords of the Congregation, had appointed themselves leaders of the anti-French protestant party. They aligned themselves with John Knox and other religious reformers. They raised 12,000 troops to oust the French from Scotland. In 1560 a treaty was signed and the French left, enabling the reformation to take effect. Scotland officially became a protestant country.

Leith sailors and Edinburgh merchants sailed regularly to the Baltic ports. These were an early centre of the Lutheran Church. It was through the traders of Leith that Luther's books, carefully concealed in bales of merchandise, were imported into Scotland despite the prohibitions against them. In this way Leith and Edinburgh made early acquaintance with protestant doctrines.

Chapter 8

The War Between Edinburgh and Leith

The quarry holes between Leith and Edinburgh – 26th June 1571

"Funny sort of day so far," said young Tom. He yawned, his scrawny frame relaxed against the tree trunk, taking in the warm sun.

"You're right there," Big Albert laughed.

Tom stretched out his legs and fingered the matchlock musket that lay beside him.

"A few hours ago, we were mustering at the Shore thinking it will be another typical day in the King's army. Bit of blade practice then off to the alehouse. Next thing we are marching up the Eastern Road to do battle."

"Aye," said Fergus, his generous mouth forcing a smile across his pointed jaw.

Fergus Preston slipped off his leather jerkin and laid it by his blade and battered helmet. He wiped his forehead with his shirt sleeve although he knew that the dripping sweat wasn't to do with the heat from the sun. He noticed his hands trembled slightly. He took a long deep breath and tensed them to make it stop. The whispers first arrived during the night, around midnight when he was still awake.

Big Albert stood up and peered across the ponds to the gathered enemy.

“And it’s only an hour ago we were shitting ourselves looking as if we were about to do battle with that Edinburgh mob. That mad bastard Captain McGregor looked as if he would explode, he seemed so wound up; forget the enemy – I thought he was going to take a swing for me.”

Fergus heard more whispers at two, three, also five and six. It was like he had a premonition. As if they sensed something was happening today.

Albert lifted his Halberd and checked its sharpness.

“And now it looks like a day sitting in the sun,” he said, his chubby face breaking into a wide grin.

Fergus nodded and through his straggly beard forced another smile that never reached his anxious blue eyes. He shivered. The whispers had stayed with him. There when he had dressed and also later when using sand to clean his sword. Food had come around but Fergus couldn’t eat a single mouthful. He tightened his jaw. It’s this waiting he hated, the wondering what was going to happen next. This had always been the worst part.

He remembered a time when he loved all this. The fight and then resting until the next one. Back for more. Resting and then back again, invariably getting away with it. But once a sabre had taken a slice of him. Then that time when that musket ball had hit the buckle of his sword belt, right over his heart, that should have been him. The memory of his younger brother crept in among the whispers. He could remember Michael's smile. Only a mile along the road from here by the Firth. But that was in a different war. Captain McGregor now held him up to the others as an example of a great fighter. Maybe once, but not anymore.

“Wonder what we would be doing if Lord Morton hadn't conscripted us? This isn’t so bad as we thought,” said Tom.

"Bet we would be knocking our pan in digging in the fields or working at the salt pans." Albert chuckled. "Or else at the Shore trying to rebuild the pier. See the state of it, it's falling to bits."

The King's army that now arrayed around the quarry holes formed twelve months before. The civil war between the Catholic followers of Mary, the Queen of Scots and the Protestant supporters of her son, the young King, had been dragging on for a year now. It didn't look like any resolution was coming soon. Apart from the officers and a few professional regulars like Fergus the army was a hotchpotch of former Leith shipwrights, maltmen, fleshers, coopers, masons, porters, and weavers. All now drilled into an effective fighting unit after months of training.

"The daft thing is my cousin Oswald is probably over the other side," said Albert. "His part of our family was always on the Queen's side. Our old dad and my Uncle Charlie had a big fall out over it with my uncle being a deacon in the Catholic church. I remember when I was wee, we all used to eat together once a month. Uncle Charlie had a tavern on the Shore back then until it burnt down when Lord Hertford invaded." He gave a little snort. "'Come back to the true religion', he would say, 'You will be a Christian and not a heretic'." he mimicked his uncle's gravelly voice. "'We must obey our priests; they draw their message from the vicar of Christ in Rome. The saints intervene in our lives, and what about the salvation of your soul?' Then our dad would pipe up."

He snickered at the memory.

"But what about the priests, their corruption and their screwing both the poor and any girl they can get their hands on?" Albert suddenly looked rueful.

"We thought it all a bit of fun back then. Certainly isn't now."

The deep breaths had helped Fergus. He felt his heartbeat becoming more regular.

"Your dad was right," he said. "Lord Morton's such a ruthless bastard I know we will win in the end."

The afternoon dragged on, the sun warm, the air barely moving, the only sound the gentle rustle of leaves in the trees. The quiet mutterings of their three hundred comrades spread out along the crest of the slope on the Leith side of the quarry holes. The Queen's infantry stood along the base of the slope that led up to the Abbey.

Fergus had become a professional soldier with Lord Morton after his time with the Lords of the Congregation protestant army that fought the French occupation ten years back. As a boy he had even fought against Herford's invasion, not that it was much of a fight. It had seemed the sensible thing if you were from Leith, given that Morton was going to base himself there. Tom and Albert were conscripted, former farm hands. It wasn't too bad; at least you got fed. Fergus saw that the two younger lads enjoyed the high jinks with their comrades, and so far, they had avoided any real action.

The whispers had returned that afternoon. They crept up on him. They made no noise, so he never saw them coming. If he had, he might have been able to make them stop. But there was never any warning.

"What's happening up there anyway?" said Tom.

Fergus shielded his eyes from the sun and peered across the ponds.

"Their army looks like they're waiting around, same as us. Our Lord Morton and their Lord Huntly seem to be doing a lot of waving their arms and stomping about looking annoyed. Same as the last time I looked. There's another bloke there with a red hat."

"Oh, he's Sir William Dury, the English ambassador – think he's helping sort things out," said Albert.

A murmur moved along the line. "Mad McGregor is coming, look lively."

Captain McGregor led Tom, Albert and Fergus's unit. There wasn't a man among them who didn't know that he was someone you didn't cross. Lean, tough and broad, with a confident swagger, thick set and fierce. Anyone could tell he was a professional soldier. His dark leather tunic was well-polished along with his Italian style helmet. He seemed to have a permanent sarcastic smile on his broad face which mirrored the angle of the deep scar across his forehead.

"Gather round and listen up boys," his voice loud and clear. "You will be glad to hear we, at last, have an agreement – both their lordships have agreed to back off; we are to return to Leith; them back to the castle," he said pointing up the hillside.

"The problem is neither of them want to leave the field first. I'm told they are worried about losing face." He gave a thin smile at their stupidity.

"So, it's agreed that the third lord, him on the horse with the red cap, when he throws his hat in the air, that's the agreed signal for both armies to leave at the same time."

"So," he said looking around the group, "what are we going to do?"

All the men were aware from experience that to give the wrong answer could lead to their nose having a meeting with McGregor's fist. All were therefore wary of giving any reply for fear it was the wrong one.

"Return to Leith," said a voice from the rear.

McGregor's face reddened, as his expression hardened. "Return to Leith? There is no chance we are letting these popish bastards off the hook. Now listen here, you useless bunch of peasants, gather in close and listen very, very carefully." There was a note of aggression in his voice.

"What Lord Morton has instructed is this. What we are going to do is…"

*

The tension among the men was palpable. Everyone made a final check of their equipment. Tom and Albert stood together, Albert's huge fame in sharp contrast with the skinny, wiry Tom. Fergus could see the excitement in their faces. They were young, inexperienced. He turned and eyed the Queen's army at the base of the Abbey Hill.

The whispers had crept closer, like a cat stalking a mouse. Then Fergus knew they were immediately behind him. Then they just leant forward and whispered in his ear. They tapped him on the shoulder. They spoke about the million things he wanted to do in his life. The million things still to say. But that he was bound to get it eventually. And then he would be a corpse. The whispers told him what he would look like, the blood, the twisted broken body with its contorted face.

In the distance, Sir Dury threw his hat in the air.

Captain McGregor kept his voice low. "Soon as they go over the ridge we are going straight after them; we will hit them hard boys, hit them hard."

Fergus felt himself shaking. *There's an entire world where people are living their lives and not getting killed. I'm the one that's going to get killed and I don't want to die. Oh God, I don't want to die, not today.*

With a clink of metal, the Queen's men made a neat turn and wheeled around on their way up over the top of the hill and down towards the Abbey. The King's army turned, marched twenty steps, then turned again.

As soon as the last Queen's man had gone over the lip of the hill Morton raised his sword and McGregor gave the word to run forward. Fergus turned and looked at Tom and Arthur. Their eyes met, and Fergus could see their fear and excitement.

They ran to the top of the ridge, in line formation. All three hundred reached the crest then slowed. Then the pace quickened as they came over the top. Below, the Queen's men were walking nonchalantly in broken formation as if out for an afternoon stroll.

With Morton's men having surprise and the higher ground it was a massacre.

The whispering stopped as Fergus charged down the hill. A wave of adrenaline seared through his body. Tom knelt and fired. The first man fell. The Queen's men didn't know which way to turn and were in disarray – some stood to fight but most stumbled and tripped their way downhill, desperate to reach the safety of the Abbey.

Fergus killed a man with a thrust of his sword. He felt the bloodlust. McGregor screamed at their head as he led the charge downhill. Fergus saw a man's twisted face as he slashed at him. A scream as the blood ran across his breeches. Fergus stabbed and then slashed and then stabbed again at men whose faces screwed up in shock and fear.

Minutes later it was over. Dead and wounded lay along the road to the Canongate. Some were prisoners, others had made it to safety behind Edinburgh's walls.

*

In the twilight they made a triumphant march back to Leith. Tom and Albert were euphoric, chatting excitedly, going over the day's events and sharing stories with their comrades. On the Shore they received a hero's welcome. Torches were lit, ale flowed and jigs were danced in a night of celebration. They had mocked their prisoners as they crammed them into the dungeons of the port's fine new Tolbooth – including Albert's cousin Oswald.

Late that night the three comrades staggered and swayed their way up Carpet Lane on the way to their billet.

"Funny sort of day," slurred Tom.

"Aye, it was that," said Albert as he swayed across the cobbles.

Fergus didn't slur or sway; he said nothing, and thought about the next time.

Historical Note

The skirmish at the quarry holes became known as "Black Saturday" and was part of the civil war which broke out in 1570. This was between the Catholic supporters of Mary Queen of Scots who wanted her returned to the throne (from which she had been forced to abdicate) following her imprisonment in England, and the Protestants who recognised her son James VI (and later I of England) as their sovereign. The war lasted three years.

Lord Morton soon became the fourth regent of young King James I of England/VI of Scotland and for a time based his government in Leith at Parliament Square. He was executed 10 years later, beheaded with the "Maiden" a guillotine that can be seen in the National Museum of Scotland. This was due to his involvement in the murder of Darnley (Mary Queen of Scots second husband)

The quarry holes were water-filled ancient quarries positioned northeast of Calton Hill and near the present-day Hillside crescent. You can still see traces of quarry mounds among trees in Royal Terrace/London Road.

Leith Tolbooth was built around 1565 and was demolished in 1829 despite attempts by Sir Walter Scott to preserve the building.

Chapter 9

The Unwelcome Visitors

Water Street, Leith – 6th June 1622

Isabel Preston scowled.

That big sapphire brooch Agnes is wearing; she's got money that one.

She glared as Agnes gave a final wave and turned down Tolbooth Wynd towards the Shore with her young son Toby in tow. Isabel noticed Nicholas's eyes following her. It was blatantly obvious he was admiring her languid stride and fine figure.

Nicholas shut the front door. Isabel coloured; she felt her blood rising. She finished chopping the cabbage, adding it to the cooking pot on the hearth of the cramped single room.

"I saw the way you smiled at that trollop," she said, ice in her voice.

Nicholas looked taken aback, surprise on his chubby face. His bushy eyebrows narrowed. "I… I … look," he stammered, "it's the first time I've seen her for ages; we used to be neighbours here before I met you. She's been away for seven years."

Given Isobel's expression he positioned his large frame to make sure the table was between them.

"I was just being friendly."

Isobel glowered; her emotions were now in so much turmoil she couldn't bring herself to say it. "Friendly my arse," she snapped. "That woman is not, and never will be welcome in our house." Isobel moved closer and brought her finger to within an inch of Nicholas's nose; her strong chin jutted, her keen green eyes livid. "If you look at her like that again I'll have your balls on a platter," she spat.

Nicholas gulped. Isobel could be fiery; this would not go away quietly. Isobel turned and prepared to leave. She put her white coif over her long fair hair and tucked it in, then lifted a blue woollen cloak over her linen shift. She picked up baby Joseph, wrapped a blanket round him and opened the door.

"I'm going to the market on the shore, you better get out your tools and start mending that broken chest," she said pointing. "You promised me weeks ago, I want it done by the time I come back." She stomped out onto the street with a face like thunder and slammed the door so hard that the whole house shook. Isobel headed briskly past Lamb the merchant's fine new home and was about to turn down Broad Wynd when she heard a popping noise. She stopped. *What was it?* You would almost think it sounded like musket shot, and where might it be coming from?

A sudden loud thud behind her, followed by a massive bang. The sound of breaking glass, a splintering of wood, masonry falling, billowing dust filled the street and then screams. She turned, shaking. Only fifty yards away the whole wall of the narrow wooden tenement next to her own had collapsed, flames licking up from the wreckage. Her neighbour Big Angus came rushing out into the street still holding the fishing net he had been mending.

"What is it, what's happening?" he shouted.

"Are we at war?" shrieked Isobel.

"I don't know," cried Angus. "What's going on?"

Dozens of people spilled onto the street in terror. The whistle of another ball came flying overhead, then the explosion as it landed in the field beyond. Sporadic musket fire echoed around the houses, but from where?

Trying not to panic, Isobel held little Joseph close and ran away from the blaze down Broad Wynd. She charged to the bottom of the muddy lane. On arriving at the Shore, she nearly fell over, stunned by the scene before her. All along the quayside porters, beggars, housewives, children and merchants cowered behind the bales of wool, and rows of barrels. Wine flowed like a tap on the cobbles with so many barrels holed. She felt a stab of horror. A few yards in front of her she saw a man and a child lying dead, sprawled on the stone slabs by the river's edge, the wine mixing with their blood.

At the mouth of the harbour three large ships poured cannon fire into each other at close range. A thick smoke drifted across the wharf mingling with the thin drizzle. The stink of powder overpowered the usual rotting fish, sewage and seaweed. Isobel gasped as a man fell from the rigging of the ship closest to her.

She ran for the cover of an upturned longboat by the wall of the Kings Wark and scrabbled underneath with Joseph. She wasn't the first; others crowded the space.

"What on earth is going on?" she asked the two porters cowering beside her. "Who are we fighting?"

The grizzled looking older one pointed through the small gap under the boat. "Yesterday that Spanish Galleon came in to take on supplies but this morning these two Dutchman, the big Carrack and the Carvel came into the harbour and attacked them."

"It looks as if they have decided to carry on their war right on our doorstep," said the younger.

"So, what will happen, is anyone doing anything about it?" screeched Isobel, struggling to keep the fear out of her voice.

The older man nodded. "Aye they have sent up to the castle."

Sporadic firing continued. Isobel lay cowering, her arms wrapped around Joseph. She took several deep breaths, bringing her panic under control. She looked around. Next to the pair of porters knelt two old fish wives who had the good sense to bring their baskets under the boat with them. As her eyes moved further along, she jerked in surprise. At the far end was Agnes with her son Toby. Her mind went into a spin and she shivered. Not only was she caught up in this terrifying situation but now she would have to spend the next god knows how long in proximity to the woman she knew she detested despite them never having spoken.

Tense, she tried to get her thoughts into some kind of order.

The pungent smell of tobacco smoke started to fill the enclosed space as one porter lit a pipe. The strange habit had become popular with men in the port over the past few years. She coughed; her eyes watered in the haze. Joseph began to cry.

Half an hour passed. The mayhem continued at the mouth of the harbour. Isobel squinted at Agnes and Toby from the corner of her eye. Agnes wore a fine-looking blue gown, dark hair and high cheekbones, a handsome woman. Yes, Isobel was now even more certain, there was no doubt in her mind that her theory was correct.

The firing outside slowed. Then the clip clop of horses and the rumble of wheels as a cannon trundled onto the quayside followed by the stomping of boots from the direction of Tolbooth Wynd. Isobel peeked out from under the boat. A troop of around fifty of the king's men had swept onto the Shore, smart and well-ordered, with grey tunics and cloaks, black breeches tied at the knee with a ribbon holding up their white stockings and dark blue wide-brimmed hats. A few carried Matchlock muskets, others axes or pikes. They took the cannon from its limber and rolled it to the edge of the wharf, the men fanned out on both sides of the river. The firing petered out and then stopped. For ten minutes all went quiet, a tense silence. The tide now out, the three ships sat immovable on the mud bottom of the sand bar that crossed the harbour mouth.

The two fishwives scrambled out; the others followed. Isobel tried to move back towards Broad Wynd but with a rattle of his musket a soldier firmly told her to stay where they were. She turned; Agnes was behind her. She said something Isobel chose not to hear and moved to the river's edge.

One of the King's officers, with the aid of a speaking trumpet, called to the ships. They responded and a few minutes later Isobel watched as two small boats dropped onto the river, then a rising and falling of oars as they approached the quay. Two captains climbed the ladder. Soldiers moved into a tight protective formation around them as their senior officer waited. A crowd had gathered. Holding Joseph with care Isobel pulled herself onto a barrel to see what was happening.

The Spanish captain was tall and thin. He had a hook nose with a drooping moustache, dressed in an expensive looking green jerkin and white canvass doublet.

"Don Pedro de Vanroz at your service." He gave an exaggerated bow; Isobel could see he was nervous. The Dutch captain was squat and broad, scruffy by comparison, wearing a cap with a thick grubby cotton waistcoat under his canvas jacket.

"Mynheer de Hautin, Admiral of the Dutch fleet."

Isobel thought his wide features had the look of a cat examining its prey.

It soon became clear that Don Pedro, realising he was trapped was demanding guarantees of safe passage. Animated haggling continued between the captains and the king's officer, the Spaniard gesticulating wildly.

The throng of Leithers was becoming restless, a growing anger at the damage done. Several people killed. The full length of the Shore, glass broken and masonry damaged, some smaller boats sunk. The soldiers had to raise their weapons to hold the mob back. Shouts from the locals demanded recompense, and from a few hotheads came calls for revenge. It was clear to Isobel the Leithers were on the Dutch side. After the wars of the past the port was a protestant stronghold; Spanish Catholics were not welcome.

Below her in the crowd Isobel studied Agnes and her son more closely. Those eyes, that hair. Agnes glanced up at her and smiled. Isobel looked away, frowning. The three men shook hands and nodded in agreement that the Spaniards would leave unmolested. The sun was dipping as the captains rowed back to their ships to the jeers of the locals. With the tide rising, the ships could soon move. Troops on the Shore remained alert and in position.

Spanish sailors pulled on ropes and halliards; their sails rose. The ship began to turn.

Bang!

Isobel almost fell from her vantage point at the sudden cannon shot. Smoke billowed from the leading Dutch Galleon. There was a sound of splitting wood as the ball smashed into the Spaniard's stern. Isobel along with everybody else dived back for cover – all hell was let loose as again all three ships opened fire. The king's canon joined the fray. Smoke and a powerful scent of gunpowder filled her nostrils as it swept over the quayside; explosions, musket fire, and screams.

Isobel peeked from behind the barrel. Flames came from the Spanish ship as it swung round out of control, its rudder shot away. It drifted on the flooding tide. Its steering gone, it listed and crashed into the black rocks by the harbour mouth.

The Dutch moved forward and increased their rate of fire; the Spanish offered no resistance. Its back broken, fire licked up the mast, the ship started to break up on the boulders. Men jumped as the flames spread onto the sails; some drowned, others paddled and staggered the short distance to the water's edge. The mob surged forward. The line of soldiers on the shore held briefly then broke, allowing the Leithers to attack the unfortunate men and strip them of anything of worth. Fire engulfed the ship, lighting up the darkening sky. Then, as suddenly as they had arrived the Dutch hoisted their sails, turned together on the rising tide and headed back out to sea.

An hour later darkness had fallen. The Spanish ship continued burning, its smashed frame dying on the black rocks. On the quayside stalls with hot drinks and food were prepared. The Shore was still crowded, everyone in a daze or stunned, but no one wanted to leave as they shared the day's amazing events. Talk was animated, damage examined, temporary repairs made, bodies removed.

Nicholas had at last got through the cordon of soldiers. He was in a panic. *Where might they be? Had they been injured in the battle?* There was only one subject among the jabbering throng as he tried to fight his way through. War had come to Leith, for the first time in a generation since his old, long dead Grandad Fergus's time.

In his search Nicholas turned up Broad Wynd. His jaw dropped when he saw Isobel by the food stall. It fell further when he saw Agnes sitting beside her with Joseph asleep in her arms, Toby at their feet eating a sausage. Isobel smiled sweetly.

"Oh Nicholas, what excitement we have had today, where have you been?"

Nicholas stood speechless.

"And you know Agnes, and little Toby here," she patted the boy on the head. "Your son."

Historical Note

Lamb's House in Water Street was built in 1610 and is the oldest surviving building in Leith.

The black rocks lie under where the Scottish office building now stands.

This incident was part of the 30 years' war between the Dutch and Spanish(1619–1648).

Chapter 10

The Walk

Leith Walk – 7th August 1650

Maggie wiped her hands on her grimy woollen smock and laid the cloth out on the grass. She spilled their meagre rations from her bag. Two large loaves of bread, a chunk of mouldy cheese and the pitcher of ale, all issued from the quartermasters that morning. The sun shone. A light breeze ruffled the long dark hair that framed her pale elfin features. She glanced up. Her big hazel eyes again met with Joseph's. This time she didn't look away but held his gaze.

Joseph Preston smiled and eventually turned away as he stood up. Tall and long-limbed in a filthy Hodden grey uniform, his long, fair hair in a ponytail, handsome; with high cheekbones and the confident air of someone in charge. He stepped back and looked along the earthen breastwork wall and ditch that stretched into the distance up towards Edinburgh.

"Hard to believe we have finished it," he said with a smile.

There was a light atmosphere among the work squad today as they sat along the base of the embankment, even laughter, despite their bedraggled state. Under ordinary circumstances, they would have appeared an unusual mix – youthful weavers, wealthy old women, ancient sailors and grizzled hat makers. Their paths could rarely be expected to cross but now every one of them shared a sense of achievement.

In an automatic response, they ducked at the muffled sound of cannon fire in the distance, two rounds in quick succession. The whistle of the balls, the ground shuddered when with a thump they landed on the other side of the breastworks.

"But best we still keep our heads down," Joseph laughed uneasily.

Then came a much louder noise as a canon from their side of the parapet responded, and again, matching the fire from Cromwell's army arrayed well to the south.

All along the wall similar groups had laboured together over the past months. A gargantuan effort by the people of Leith to build the defences required to enable General Leslie to keep Cromwell's invaders at bay.

Maggie lay on the grass, her wee brother Alec alongside her. Joseph, work squad leader and a corporal in General Leslie's forces sat with the others. It was his eyes that attracted Maggie, a dark gunmetal grey yet warm, spirited and sharp.

In contrast, next to him sat big Ian McDonald—all muscle and saliva—who ran a blacksmith shop in Burgess street. Since Maggie made it clear that his advances were unwelcome, he seemed to go out of his way to make her life difficult. He was one of the most irritating men Maggie had ever met.

Big Ian stuffed a bit of bread in his mouth. "Alec," he said with his usual stupid grin, "I'll give you a shilling if you walk on the top of the wall all the way to Edinburgh."

"All right," squeaked Alec as he started to hoist himself up, struggling with his withered hand and twisted leg up the sloping earthwork.

Maggie bristled and stood up quickly, her lithe frame tense. "Alec," she screamed, "get yourself back down here this instant!"

Alec looked confused for a second before reversing his movements. Big Ian laughed.

"And as for you," shouted Maggie turning on him. "You fat pig, I've had enough of you taking the rise out of him; if you so much as say a word to him again, I'll slap you so hard."

Ian's smile vanished; a look of malevolence crossed his wide beefy face. "Don't you talk to me like that you little bitch." He rose, raised his fist and moved towards her.

In a quick, fluid movement Joseph was on his feet. He grabbed the big man's wrist, twisted his arm up his back and tripped him, sending him spiralling into a puddle with a muddy splash. The blacksmith lifted himself up spluttering, soaking and filthy. He turned to face Joseph, rage in his eyes. Joseph raised his fists. McDonald eyed the two of them, Joseph's cool demeanour contrasting sharply with Maggie, her eyes blazing and hot tears of anger running down her face.

He spun, stomping away with a face like thunder. There was silence in the group as he strode off.

"We have done our work for the day," announced Joseph casually. The tension lifted and the light atmosphere returned as they all rose and started in the direction of the town's western gate, keeping their heads lowered.

"I'll walk you back," said Joseph turning to Maggie.

Maggie turned without answering. "Come on Alec, we are going home."

*

The mood in the port was optimistic despite the war. General Leslie had assembled a force of forty thousand men and mobilised the entire town to build a defensive breastwork which now ran the full length in a straight line right up to Edinburgh. Extensive work had been done to reinstate the walls from one hundred years before when the French had occupied. For the past month Cromwell's forces had been trying to drive their way through but the defences held. The latest gossip was Cromwell was organising a retreat, and also now a rumour that General Leslie would break out and chase him back across the border.

Joseph and Maggie walked in silence, only broken by Alec's occasional meaningless chatter.

"Tell me about your family," said Joseph as they ambled at a gentle pace to allow Alec to keep up.

"I … we … we had a part share in a ship." She fell silent. "Tell me about yours."

"My father Nicholas was a carpenter in Mr Coustean's shipyard, but he was a clever man and so became a preacher. He was a staunch supporter of the new religion."

As they came along Tolbooth Wynd Joseph stopped and flicked a coin to a young beggar, a bad infection in both his legs.

"He strongly believed the king was trying to force Catholicism upon us. And he was a strong opponent of it. He also understood the protestant church had to reform and was among the first to sign the Covenant."

On the Shore some shops and stalls were still open. Until recently supplies had been getting through. On offer were beer and vegetables and even a bit of meat.

"He became an important man once the English civil war started; they involved him with negotiating for us Scots to fight alongside the Parliament forces. He thought by supporting Cromwell he could achieve the protestant freedoms he believed in. We were together in the army that fought with him against King Charles at the battle of Marston Moor."

Maggie's brows furrowed. "It's all so confusing. So, back then we were on the same side as Cromwell but now we have Scottish protestants fighting English protestants, and we Scots are supporting the King again. I just don't understand it, Joseph, not at all."

"You see, over time we realised Cromwell was a dictator. When he beheaded King Charles, it was a step too far and we also fell out when it became obvious he would not help us reform the church how we wanted."

Maggie stopped at a booth and bought oats, bread, a cabbage and a jug of ale.

"Tell me of your family, and why a woman as attractive as you is not married."

Maggie looked away. "I don't want to talk of that."

Despite the war the port had remained active until a few weeks before when Cromwell ships came into the Forth. Now nothing could move. The harbour was busy; a Bark, two Hulks, and a big Carrack lined the quay. However, rather than the usual bustle the only sound was a few pennants and ropes flapping in the wind along with the murmur from the handful of sailors lounging on the decks with little to do. One was splicing a piece of frayed cordage, the others played dice.

They came up Broad Wynd to Maggie's wooden tenement in Water Street.

"This is home."

Joseph smiled, bowed and made to leave.

"Come up," said Maggie, her cheeks reddening, "for a drink."

She turned to Alec. "Alec, stay here and watch the sailors on their ships. I know how much you like that, sitting by the river and seeing the boats." She pointed him towards the Shore. "Come home when it gets dark."

Alec giggled, happy to have the opportunity for one of his favourite pastimes.

Maggie's spartan home was on the second floor of the timber fronted block. Over time rooms had been subdivided or additional rooms tacked on to what had become a rabbit warren. There was a stink from the midden at ground level. She had two rooms, one for sleeping and the other with three stools and a small table in front of a single window with shutters. On the walls clumps of sweet-smelling herbs. A spinning wheel stood in the corner.

She poured ale into earthenware mugs; their eyes met. Joseph looked at her, and she at him. They moved closer together; they kissed.

*

An hour and a half later as they dressed Maggie realised she felt happier than she had for years.

"Alec," she paused, "is all I have left."

"What happened?" said Joseph softly.

"The plague, five years ago."

"We were away south with Cromwell at the time. I heard it was bad."

Maggie's muscles tightened in her chest.

"It took my parents, six of my brothers and sisters and nine of my aunts, uncles, and cousins. We lost everything. It was a terrible time."

"Can't be something that's easy to forget."

"It happened so quickly. My dad decided we should go but then my sister fell ill so Mother wouldn't leave her, then my two brothers got it and so we were forced into quarantine in a hut on the Links with the others who were infected. So, by then it was too late, we couldn't go anyway."

She looked up at Joseph.

"Then they just went. One by one."

She wiped the tear forming in her eye.

"It wasn't only us. Over half the people in Leith died; dead lying in the streets, no one to remove the bodies."

Joseph moved forward and held her. Maggie's lips trembled, then she cried, for the first time in five years.

*

Afternoon turned into evening. Maggie prepared a cabbage and fish stew. They ate, and talked.

"It's getting dark, Alec should be home by now. Let's go and find him; he would lose his head if it wasn't screwed on."

"Maggie," said Joseph. "Will you marry me?"

Maggie glanced up. She smiled and let out a long sigh. "Come on, let's find Alec; we can talk about that later."

She took his hand and led him down the stairs. At the Shore Alec was nowhere to be found. They checked in the taverns and walked the narrow alleyways calling his name. They asked the neighbours. It appeared that nobody had seen him.

The young beggar with the infected legs lay in the same spot as earlier. He told them he had spotted Alec with the big man who ran the blacksmiths around the corner, walking back up towards the western gate. Maggie and Joseph made their way up quickly. They passed the guards at the gate. Two hundred yards further up the wall they could see the light from a cluster of torches. They hurried towards a group of soldiers. On the ground at the base of the barrier lay a body. Joseph took a torch and lowered it. Maggie's expression turned to one of horror. It was Alec, his body broken and twisted.

"We tried to stop him but he said he had to walk all the way to Edinburgh," said a soldier.

Maggie's heart sank, she felt her knees buckle. She let out the cry of a wounded animal.

Joseph drew out his knife, and went hunting.

Historical Note

A few weeks later General Leslie did pursue Cromwell but was defeated at the battle of Dunbar. Cromwell then entered Leith and Edinburgh unopposed. His occupation lasted ten years.

The plague of 1645 was the worst in Leith's history. It's estimated that 2,700 people died out of a population of 4–5,000.

The earth rampart and ditch built by Leslie eventually developed into Leith Walk. By 1706 the author Daniel Defoe described it as a "very handsome gravel walk, twenty feet broad". For a time, wheeled transport was forbidden – hence "walk".

The Covenant was a document which rejected the attempts by King Charles to impose English religious practices in Scotland. The Scots were anxious to preserve their religious identity. The Covenanters became a significant force over a long period of upheaval and civil war in Scotland.

Chapter 11

The Gibbit

Water Street, Leith – 28th August 1678

"**Y**ou have big strong hands, Rab," the Constable had said yesterday.

Marion Preston knew Rab well enough to tell that since then he had been as nervous as she had ever seen him. He had spent all morning stomping round their spartan top floor single room; he could not settle. She sensed today was not going to be easy for him.

Rab sat his large frame on the big bench, got up, crossed the room and sat on the wee bench, stood up again and returned to his breakfast. Being such a big man, it was hard for Marion to hide her exasperation given what was, despite their meagre possessions, a cramped space, but she made sure not to show it.

Marion sensed his anxiety; today she just had to support him through it. She had taken care to avoid the subject when they rose at dawn. Since then she had kept herself busy, got the children up and dressed in their best wool smocks, emptied the night soil out the window, started a fire to heat the big pot, and swept the floor.

"Big day," said Marion.

"Aye," said Rab, his eyes focussed on his pottage as he moved it around the wooden bowl with a piece of bread. It would soon be time for him to leave; he had barely touched the food – usually he would have scoffed the lot in the space of a few seconds. The children, Annie and wee Edward chattered, squirmed and annoyed each other in their usual way, not picking up on the tension so apparent to Marion. Normally, Rab would have skelped them on the head by now, but not today; his task distracted him.

"You should eat something."

"Aye," replied Rab as he continued to play with his food.

They sat in silence, even the youngsters quietened.

Marion spoke softly. "I am right proud of you, Rab. There will be hundreds of folk there."

"You'll be lucky if you lot can see anything," he said as he shifted in his seat. He gently swept back Annie's unruly hair. "You will need to be there early."

After breakfast Marion pulled Rab's most prized piece of clothing from the big chest. She had spent most of the previous evening cleaning and brushing it until it almost looked like new. She helped Rab put on the red coat – the uniform of the guard. Marion was aware they were lucky; not only did Rab now have a secure job and a regular wage but people seemed to respect him as he patrolled the town with this red jacket and cudgel. He was built for the part, a huge man over six feet tall, barrel chested and broad shouldered. Thick forearms. A ruddy complexion on his wide face, long, wavy fair hair falling over his high forehead.

They thought he might have got the job because when a laddie he fought with the Covenanters.

When they first met, he worked as a labourer at the harbour. Her uncle knew the right people and put in a good word, and next thing they called him to the Tolbooth to sign up. They couldn't believe their luck.

With his size and strength, the role wasn't difficult for Rab. The harbour was the focus of his work, much of it helping the Baillies make sure that nobody fiddled the taxes on what came into the port. With around forty ships a year arriving it was doing well; wool, hides and dried fish going out and wine, olive oil and other luxuries brought in.

Apart from the harbour all he had to deal with was the occasional domestic, the odd fight in the taverns and keeping the town beggars and rabble in order. Usually he only needed to swing his cudgel a few times and most people soon understood the message. It was rare that he had to use it when dragging any miscreants off to jail.

"Right," said Rab raising his big frame, "I better get down to the Tolbooth."

"Good luck, I know you will do well." She pecked his stubbled cheek.

There had been grumbles from neighbours; a few thought he was supporting the money grabbing Edinburgh Magistrates but that had been a problem for as long as anyone could remember, and nobody was ever stupid enough to try and challenge him directly. Marion and Rab didn't have any issue with that so long as they paid him. Another benefit was that he was able to turn a blind eye to any smuggling by his local friends and Marion well knew that this was likely to be a lucrative sideline to be developed in the future. Yes, she realised, things were looking up, maybe they could soon afford to rent a nice cottage over the bridge in North Leith, away from the stink.

Today Rab had a different kind of task – what's more, he would receive a large bonus for the work. Rab was lucky in that the man usually brought in from Musselburgh for the job was ill with the flux.

With Rab gone Marion sat with the children, her generous mouth and rosy cheeks framed by a frayed bonnet from which strands of dark hair drifted. She combed Annie's hair and wiped Edward's grubby face, preparing for the day's outing. Despite the extra money, Marion had a bad feeling about Rab's task. He was to do the deed itself; it gave her a queasy sensation – and as for this whole Patsy Brown thing, it still left a nasty taste somehow. Who would have believed it?

A pang of sadness run through her. Rab's poor mum Maggie, what a way to die. After what she had been through in her youth, losing her entire family in the plague and then her husband at the Battle of Dunbar only to later discover she was pregnant with Rab. The Patsy Brown affair had been troubling Marion during most of her waking moments for the last few weeks as the whole story came to light.

A knock on the door, it opened and her sister Judith rushed in, dressed in her best beige woollen bodice and skirt over a newly washed white linen shift. A tremble of excitement was on her full lips, her long dark hair combed and adorned with red ribbons. She took up the conversation at the very place Marion's thoughts had left it.

"Oh, I hear Rab's been chosen for the job. May the Lord protect us," said Judith dramatically, and put her hands to her lips as if praying. "So, it's true, who could believe it, it's such a shock," she said excitedly

She opened her arms and raised her eyes skywards.

"The Devil is in our midst; he has even killed Rab's mother. Thank the Lord we have the church to protect us."

Marion said nothing. Her expression showed she was unimpressed at Judith's dramatic performance.

"So, what's the latest, have you heard anything else?" said Judith frowning, put out that her dramatics had not had the desired effect.

Marion was wary of her sister. She had never trusted her, even when they were youngsters. She had always been sneaky. And then a year ago that incident at the village fayre when she found her and Rab in a drunken clinch in an alleyway round the back of the Old Ship hotel. Their relationship had never been the same since. She made such a drama out of everything and Marion didn't like how enthusiastic she appeared with the whole Patsy thing, although everyone in the port was talking about nothing else so she wasn't alone in that. Marion decided that there was no point in keeping any information from her.

"Aye, Rab came in late last night from the Tolbooth, says it's a watertight case. The witch hunter arrived from Musselburgh a few days ago and carried out his tests – Patsy had the Devil's mark. Rab said she was tried by the magistrate and sentenced along with four others."

"Yes, I heard that bit," said Judith. "The minister told us that this morning, he said a whole group had been in league with the Devil for years, that's the reason for so many deaths and poor harvests over the last while. I can hardly believe it, Rab's mum's own pal…"

"Aye," said Marion. "Rab says that Patsy had been a friend of his mother since he was a wee laddie. The whole episode devastated him; he thought his mother was a good judge of character, so how could she have been so wrong about Patsy Brown?"

"What else did he tell you?" said Judith, her eyes inquisitive.

"He says he remembered as a child Patsy popping into the house. Not exactly a bundle of fun and she could be a bit of a gossip sometimes but overall, he always quite liked her. Sometimes she came around with herbs when he was ill and she even helped deliver his next-door neighbours' baby when the usual wifey was away."

Marion picked up a sack and began to fill it with fruit and cheese for the outing.

"You'll remember it was only a week after his mum's funeral when it started. The days after she died, we were all in a state of shock after the burial at the South Leith churchyard and we were trying to get back into the usual routine."

"How could I forget?" said Judith. "Did it not start when that awful family of tinkers who lived across the burn up by the preceptory ruins fell out with Patsy when she was a witness at the trial of one the tinker brothers who had assaulted and robbed a magistrate; remember, they hung him a week later? The tinker said a demon was to blame but at his trial Patsy said she knew it was a demon all right – the demon drink that is."

"That's right," said Marion. "After that one of the tinkers reported they saw her at Musselburgh as a ship had floundered and was lost with all hands. Then that wee girl who lived at Sandport died after taking Patsy's herbs. Then the farmer who used the common land behind her hovel on the edge of the village had three of his precious cattle die within a week."

"And then Rab's mother," said Judith.

"Yes, people saw Patsy and her walking down the Kirkgate together. They said that Patsy wore a mean look on her face and at the bottom of the street Rab's mum suddenly collapsed and died. Soon it wasn't only the tinkers talking about her but it was everyone in the port; before you knew it, they had arrested her and thrown her in the Tolbooth."

"It was all so strange, said Judith. "Today at least justice will be done, and it seems only fair Rab will do the killing."

*

An hour later Marion, Judith and the children met as arranged on the

Shore at the door of the Old Ship. As usual the harbour was busy. A train of packhorses had arrived so a stream of carts relayed another big consignment of wool to the warehouses. A large East Indiaman sat by the wharf causing a stir among the porters and stevedores as a cargo of silk and spices spilled onto the quayside. Marion had prepared a picnic and Judith popped into the hotel for a pot of beer to take with them. They set off upriver towards the Gallows. It was a fine day; they left the river and headed up the track towards Edinburgh. It soon became obvious that, encouraged by the weather there would be a bumper crowd. There was barely a cloud in the sky and only a light breeze. They headed up the path with hundreds of others, half the population of Leith heading the same way. The crowd was merry when they arrived at the Gallowlee. Old friends chatted and laughed, dogs scurried, ragged children with grubby feral faces and foul mouths jostled, jugglers juggled, traders set stalls out offering pies, cakes and beer – a big turnout down from Edinburgh as well.

Rab made sure of a reserved spot for them on the slope of the small hillock next to the scaffold. It was ideal, they would have a great view of the day's proceedings. The scaffold had recently been rebuilt, a platform with a long beam for the hanging and in front a thick pole stuck into the ground. They laid out a blanket and got themselves comfortable.

Then a loud cheer, a commotion as the group of witches came into sight on the path from Leith, Rab at their head. Marion experienced a surge of pride at how smart he looked. The five witches made slow progress up the rutted track, tied together at the hands and feet as they shuffled along, guards cajoling them. Marion remembered Patsy usually dressed well, but not today. Even a week in a cramped cell in Leith Tolbooth had reduced her to filthy rags. It was only because Marion recognised the colour that she was aware it was her best woollen smock.

The crowd surrounded them as they stumbled their way up the track, young boys ran back and forth shouting while an ancient woman (from the tinker family) spat on each of them in turn. Patsy was second in the line. Marion thought she looked awful. Downtrodden and in a daze. Likely the result of being beaten and starved.

She felt a stab of sympathy for her, the niggling thought at the back of her mind, it still didn't feel right somehow. Then she remembered the terrible things Patsy had done. She deserved all that was coming to her.

On the Gibbet five ropes hung from the beam. The stake in front was where Rab would earn his bonus. He gave them a wave as he spotted them. On the scaffold a black clad preacher was shouting at the mob, with a nose like a hawk and a madness in his eyes as he strutted around the stage. "They practice witchcraft, they do much evil in the eyes of the Lord," he screamed, pointing with a jabbing finger at the group.

Marion emptied her bag and laid out their picnic.

"Oh, look at Rab, isn't he so handsome," said Judith.

Marion ignored her. The preacher gesticulated wildly, aiming to drive the crowd into a frenzy. "The book of Leviticus tells that those of the spirits should be put to death, we must kill them and stone them. Their blood will be on their own heads."

Marion handed round the bread, apples and cheese with wooden cups of beer. On the light breeze smells of newly cut timber, manure from the fields and fried meat from the food stalls. Guards moved the crowd back and brought the witches to the front of the platform.

The minister was now on his knees screaming at the top of his voice with his arms raised to the heavens. "In the name of Christ our Lord, please save us from these devils."

Rab moved forward and grabbed the first of the five, an old wifey from Granton that none of them knew. Her bones were as thin as a birch sticks and her eyes glazed over, confused by what was going on around her. Rab dragged her up to the pole with ease. She whimpered. Marion from her vantage point caught a whiff of something as the old lady emptied her bowels. Rab held her in front of the stake and put the rope round her neck and began to turn the garrotte. She offered no resistance and with his huge hands he squeezed the life out of her with three quick turns. Her body went limp and the other guards pulled her onto the gallows, put a noose round her neck and hung her. The mob cheered.

"Oh, look Mum, Dad's going to do Patsy next," cried Annie her eyes wide with excitement.

"She will be harder to do than that last crone I'll bet," said Judith.

"Kill the witch!" shouted Judith.

Marion shuddered as the children joined in.

"Kill the witch!" they cried.

Rab separated Patsy and hauled her from the group to the pole. The grizzled old tinker lady stepped in front dancing demonically and spitting. Rab slapped her hard, sending her reeling into the dust. Patsy then appeared to come out of her daze as if suddenly realising her predicament and dug her heels in resistance.

"No, Rab, don't," she screamed. "I'm not a witch. I was friends with your mother, I'm not a witch, don't Rab, don't."

Patsy glanced up and caught Marion's eye. She stared at her imploringly. Marion's emotions lurched; this didn't feel right. She looked away. Rab grabbed Patsy in a head lock and dragged her towards the stake.

"Don't, Rab, no, no," she screeched hysterically, and tried to kick at his legs with her bound feet.

Rab pushed her roughly up against the pole and wound the rope round her neck.

Patsy's voice rose to fever pitch. "Naw Rab I didn't, a didn't…"

Rab gave the cord two quick turns and Patsy's squeals died away. She gasped, the sound as if air was being released from a bladder. He turned the garrotte again, and then again. Patsy's light was extinguished.

With her body limp another guard dragged her off and dangled her from the noose. A great cheer from the mob. After an hour the deed was done – five witches swung on the gallows. The preacher, now quiet, climbed up and prayed in front of each of the five for their souls. Then the magistrate mumbled a congratulation to Rab and pressed an extra three coins of silver into his hand. The crowd began to disperse. Rab, Marion, Judith and the youngsters packed up and made to amble back toward Leith.

"Oh, Rab you were brilliant," said Judith gushing. She smiled at him and touched his arm.

From behind her Marion gave Rab a stern scowl.

"What will we use this extra silver for?" said Rab, turning towards her.

Marion could see the strain on his face; was that a tear in his eye? It had not been an easy day for him.

"I could do with a better pot," she said.

"Dad, let's buy that new drink at the market," squealed Annie. "It's expensive, but supposed to make you healthy."

"What's it called?"

"I think they call it tea; we should get it for all of us, Aunt Judith as well."

"Absolutely not," said Marion. "We might then have enough for a new pot."

Historical Note

Around 2,000 people—mostly women—accused of being witches were executed in Scotland in the late 16th and 17th centuries. The main place of execution in Edinburgh was by the castle but they were also executed in Leith.

Executions in Leith were at first performed in North Leith next to the bridge and then at the Gallow Lee, a small hill just off Leith Walk (which had not yet been established as a main roadway) at Shrubhill. There are reports of nine witches being strangled and their bodies burnt to ashes in 1664, five more in 1678. The hill was removed and used as gravel to build the New town 150 years later. The ashes of those executed are in the mortar of the stones.

Chapter 12

The Match

The Shore, Leith – 12th June 1724

Was that him? Sam Preston had to glance twice. He took a step back. Oh, my goodness, yes, it was Ensign Porteous. They had met for the first time the week before at Straiton's Inn when he had gone to toss the coin. From the gossip since, Sam reckoned he had lost.

Despite the early hour there he was. Sat outside the Old Ship tavern in the sun holding a tankard and looking as if he didn't have a care in the world. Thick set with massive forearms, tall and athletic, broad shoulders and high forehead. He looked so composed given what was taking place later today. Sam knew this to be exactly the opposite of how he himself felt.

John Porteous glanced up and caught Sam's eye. He winked and pointed to the empty stool beside him.

Sam stopped, and sat. He had made a special effort today, put on his best clothes. A patterned waistcoat with white breeches to the knee and his best blue jacket. Stockings and a fine pair of buckled shoes. He had even combed his shaggy fair hair and shaved his youthful jaw.

Porteous bared his yellow teeth at him rather than smiled. His heavy stubble and bull neck strained against the collar of his fine red woollen coat. There was something incongruous. He dressed like a toff but had the face of a thug.

"We are a team, my lad," said Porteous quietly. "You and I are going to win."

Porteous then gave a low snort and stood. He swigged back his ale and then slapped Sam so hard on the shoulder he almost fell off his stool. By the time he pulled himself back up he could only watch as Porteous vanished up Broad Wynd.

What had that been about?

Sam had been apprehensive anyway. Mr McPherson had sent a message the evening before asking to see him. *What could he want?* Under the circumstances it was a summons he couldn't refuse.

Mr McPherson's home was on the North side of the river close by the Citadel. From the Shore Sam walked across the bridge and it didn't take him long to find the fine-looking house. It stood on its own on the edge of the town. On one side flowed the river, on the other stood the ruin. It cast a long shadow. Two of the gates and three of the original five bastions of Cromwell's great fortress still stood.

On entering a servant ushered him into Mr McPherson's little snuggery. McPherson was still in his nightcap, tall and stooped with sagging sallow skin, a sharp contrast with Sam's squat frame and youthful good looks. He welcomed him warmly. Sam relaxed. He proffered a seat and pointed, a spread of bread, cheese and ale placed on a small table.

"Well lad, you know the important part you have to play today," said McPherson

Sam nodded.

"You are well aware that these two gentlemen, Ensign Porteous and the Tenth Lord Elphinstone have agreed a wager of the huge sum of twenty guineas on this golf match. It's very important that as Club Captain I have to make sure I see everything to be above board."

"Yes, sir."

"You will no doubt have heard that Ensign Porteous has a bit of a reputation."

Sam wondered whether he should mention the brief meeting they had earlier but decided against it. "Yes, I... I heard he is a … eh … a character," said Sam.

"A character," said McPherson with a laugh. "A nice way to put it. Let's just say he is not someone to cross."

Sam gulped.

"Let me tell you a little story," said McPherson as he sat back in his chair

"My sister attends a church up in Edinburgh and they had advertised a vacancy for the post of a minister. Two young gentlemen, a Mr Dawson and a Mr Witherspoon applied. When the congregation voted on their choice, it became clear that there was an even split."

McPherson paused to sip his tea.

"As normal custom, the local committee of the Presbytery was asked to make the decision. They sided with Mr Dawson."

Sam nodded.

"But then Mr Witherspoon appealed to the higher authority of the church Synod. They reconsidered the ruling and overturned the Presbytery committee's earlier decision in Mr Witherspoon's favour."

McPherson stood up and moved to look out the window at the meandering river.

"All fine and well, you may think. Then things became a little fraught. There were accusations of foul play and bribery and it became quite clear that some members of the congregation were far from happy with the outcome. Word got to the local magistrate. Aware that feelings were running high he became worried that there might be trouble the following Sunday. In his wisdom he informed Ensign Porteous that in his role as a town guardsman he should go along and make sure of the peace."

He turned back to Sam.

"The following Sunday Mr Witherspoon was due to give his first sermon. However, encouraged by his supporters in the congregation, Mr Dawson arrived before Mr Witherspoon and set himself up at the pulpit and started to preach. At that very moment Ensign Porteous arrived. He then walked up the aisle and the pulpit steps. He grabbed poor Mr Dawson by the lapel and dragged him down the aisle and along the floor as if a common criminal, despite Mr Dawson's vehement protests.

Sam followed the story with interest.

McPherson raised an eyebrow. "So, what do you think happened then?"

"Well," said Sam cautiously, "I suppose he ejected Mr Dawson from the church? Must have been embarrassing."

"Yes, that's exactly what happened. The only problem being that poor Mr Dawson died a few days later from the injuries he received."

"Oh," said Sam.

"And as a side note, while Mr Porteous was outside assaulting Mr Dawson, Mr Witherspoon arrived by a side door whereupon Mr Dawson's supporters attacked him and he also died of his wounds soon afterwards. My sister reports many other men, women and children were injured in a great riot."

Mr McPherson's soft features hardened as he looked Sam in the eye.

"And what did the magistrates do? Nothing. There have, I gather been many similar incidents. It appears that Mr Porteous is untouchable. So, all I'm saying to you is—as we have selected you to be his caddie at today's match—be careful. Right," said McPherson as he clapped his hands together and gestured towards the door. "See you at Straiton's Inn at two p.m., don't be late."

By the time Sam returned over the bridge quite a crowd had started to gather on the quayside. The smell of rotting fish, seaweed and sewage was now accompanied by the aroma of grilled pork from the food vendors. Seagulls swooped and cried. The taverns on the Shore now busy. Despite feeling a degree of anxiety around the morning's developments, Sam's excitement was building. A part of him was very proud of the important part he had to play.

It was a perfect day for it. Sunny, while high above a handful of white clouds drifted on the light breeze. On the other side of the river a 100-ton Bark lay beached and heeled over to be scraped and tarred; two swans nibbled at the pile of discarded barnacles. They were among the few things moving. The harbour was at a standstill. An East Indiaman and two big Frigates sat motionless on the quayside. For once the ships were not surrounded with the usual scrum of porters and sailors. Today it was the crowds circulating around the shops and stalls.

Sam had a plate of mutton and kale at the Britannia Inn before mingling with the crowd. In among the hawkers, dogs and ragged children, booths and stalls competed with the usual quayside furniture of coiled ropes, old fish boxes, pallets and stacks of barrels. Today the market had everything. There was the stench of cows' innards next to the tang of spices. Kitchen implements alongside second-hand clothes, vegetables and sacks of oatmeal.

Sam left the bustle and made his way up Burgess Street. He passed through the usual stink of boiling whale oil from the soap works in Water Street and on up towards the Kirkgate. On reaching the foot of the street he stopped to compose himself. He took deep breaths. He had a sense of pride as he looked through the row of shady elms that stood in front of the big field. Like many others, that was now enclosed to protect the crops from wandering animals. Beyond, the golf links stretched all the way to the edge of the Forth.

He walked up the Kirkgate, a narrow street of shabby, timber fronted houses. High peaked gables jutted out over the row of dingy shops and booths below, among them his regular watering hole at Cant's Ordinary Inn. Further up, Straiton's Inn stood out; weather-beaten yet imposing with thick leaded windows. It was a respectable looking establishment compared to the shabby buildings and stinking middens that surrounded it.

Inside it was already busy. Maids ran around with trays of foaming ale and sweetmeats. Many distinguished visitors were congregating. Lord Hamilton and his entourage arrived minutes after Sam while the Earl of Morton was already there along with the Provost and magistrates.

In the main parlour toasts were being taken. It surprised Sam when he saw the two players standing together. They couldn't have been more different. While they both wore the same red coats and white breeches, the tenth Lord Elphinstone was a much smaller and wiry figure when compared with Porteous's bulk. He wore a powdered wig which dominated his thin face with its hooked nose.

Porteous looked friendly. He was smiling and shaking hands with those around him. Sam again met with Mr McPherson, by now dressed in his finery. The master of ceremonies stood and rang a bell. At once the hubbub stopped.

"The Tenth Lord Elphinstone and Ensign Porteous are to play a golf match of ten holes. A wager of twenty guineas are at stake." There was a low murmur of approval.

"Rules as laid down by the club. Note that only players and caddies may look for any lost balls. The match will begin in thirty minutes."

Porteous called to Sam and waved him over with a genial greeting. "Ah my caddie for the day," he smiled. "Please accompany me through to the clubroom to have a look at my clubs."

He turned and Sam followed. On entering, Porteous turned to shake his hand. Sam could feel the power in his grip, then a sudden severe pain as his bones were compressed as if in a vice. Porteous's expression tuned from a smile to a steely stare. He slowly moved his face close to Sam's. He breathed on him.

"You listen to me, you little shit."

Porteous had the finger of his other hand within half an inch of Sam's nose. He caught a whiff of foul breath. He sensed his bowels weaken.

"I'm going to win this game – and you," he jabbed Sam hard in the chest, "are going to help me."

Sam felt himself shaking. Porteous then moved his face even closer. To Sam's great relief he released his grip. He pulled an object out of his pocket and thrust it into Sam's throbbing hand. Sam looked down at what he at once recognised as a quality feathery golf ball; a handcrafted cowhide sphere which had been painstakingly stuffed with a whole bucket of goose feathers.

"Some feathers have been removed. Makes it too light so it won't fly as well. When you get a chance, you need to swap his ball for this."

Sam's red face was sweating

"There will be an extra shilling in it for you."

"B … b … but what if I get caught?"

In a flash Porteous grabbed Sam by the throat and brought his beefy face to within an inch of his.

"It's simple; do as I say, or I'll destroy you," he snarled. Sam could tell by his expression that there was no doubt that he meant it.

"F … fine," squeaked Sam.

Porteous released him and left the room.

Sam was shaking, He stumbled to the latrine to empty his bowels.

He took a deep breath to get his panic under control. *What could he do?* He thought of feigning illness. Then he thought of just running. A few moments later he heard the master of ceremonies calling on him. There was no way out, no choice, he needed to go through with it. He wiped the sweat from his face and prepared himself, noticing that his hand was trembling as he lifted Porteous's clubs under his arm and returned to the parlour.

Led by Mr McPherson the players, officials, caddies, and distinguished spectators walked in procession to the Links. Cheers rose from the throng milling at the first tee.

"Samuel, Samuel, cooee…"

Sam glanced up at his family in the crowd as they waved. There was his Aunt Annie and his dad Edward along with old Grandad Rab, stooped in his familiar shabby old red coat. Sam forced a smile and returned the gesture.

It was still sunny with only a light wind coming off the Firth. The golf course covered in patches of gorse and bracken which meandered among the undulating sand and patches of rough grass. In a few places cows and horses grazed. In another the local washerwomen had laid out the sheets they were bleaching to dry.

On the tee Lord Elphinstone started by hitting a fine drive down the middle.

"Longnose," said Porteous.

Sam handed him the hazel-shafted club. Porteous placed his ball on a small pile of sand. He stood still for a moment before taking up his stance. His torso twisted slowly to the right as he raised the club in the air before releasing in a smooth arc. There was a sweet-sounding crack as the beechwood head made contact with the ball. It flew straight and true and landed a few yards beyond his Lordship's. The crowd clapped.

It soon became clear that the two players were evenly matched despite their different styles and temperaments. They both had a smooth swing, Porteous more power with the long shots. Elphinstone showed a touch more finesse when it came to the Niblick, with superb accurate chips. Yet their temperaments were quite different. Lord Elphinstone's seemed to be reflected in his effortless movements, his wiry frame methodical and consistent, rarely deviating, always the same steady tempo. His expression rarely changed, a barely noticeable aristocratic sneer. Porteous was the opposite, an angry bull who attacked the course, seeming to push every ounce of energy into every shot. His face went through every expression from fierce delight to fierce anger and frustration.

Despite the differences in their approach the score remained neck and neck for seven holes. Then on the eighth Lord Elphinstone made a breakthrough as Porteous's usual steady use of the Cleek let him down when he missed a short putt. Sam noticed his eyes darken as he walked to the next hole and he shuddered.

On the second last Porteous hit yet another straight drive. Then when his Lordship's Applewood head club connected, he mishit and pulled it well to the left. It landed on the far side of a large gorse bush. A loud "Ahhh…" came from the crowd.

Porteous looked at Sam and gave an imperceptible nod of his head. Sam hurried forward and got to the gorse before Elphinstone's caddie. He spotted the ball and, using the bush for cover switched it, stuffing the Lord's original ball in his pocket. He looked at Porteous, who winked. From a difficult position Elphinstone fluffed his shot. Porteous appeared comfortable as he took the hole with a fine approach shot with his Spoon and a short putt. All square with one to go.

The crowd had now swollen and was becoming increasingly raucous as the tension rose. Sam could sense it as they walked to the last tee. By now several hundred were following them. Refreshment vendors had set up their stalls near the final hole. There was almost a carnival atmosphere.

The pressure was building; Sam could see beads of sweat on both players' foreheads as they stood on the tee. Porteous set up his stance carefully, but he snatched his shot and sliced the drive into a boggy patch on the right, his face like thunder as it reddened in frustration. Elphinstone's drive was mediocre; he connected well enough, but it didn't go far. Porteous's poor drive had cost him his advantage, and he wasted a shot having to chip out of the bog. His Lordship's second again didn't seem to have the legs and he was still well short of the hole.

Porteous then hit a fine third with his Spoon and landed within three feet of the target. Lord Elphinstone's third was again weak. It looked as if it would fall well short but then a lucky bounce brought it to within putting distance but still twenty feet away.

The players marched up to the final green. Mr McPherson stood holding the purse.

Elphinstone asked for a cow pat to be removed before he crouched for his putt. The crowd became silent.

With a firm stroke of his Cleek, Elphinstone sent the ball off at a steady pace. It was accurate but stopped short only two inches from the hole. A loud sigh went around the throng. Porteous needed only to hole the three-foot downhill putt to take the prize.

To Sam's horror, he sensed something slipping down his leg. The ball he had switched had escaped from a hole in his pocket and was slithering down the inside of his breeches. He slapped his thigh to stop it but only succeeded in sending it flying out faster. It came shooting out bottom of his breeches and it hit the toe of his shoe before rolling down the sloping grass and into the hole. Porteous looked up, fury in his eyes. Elphinstone looked up; his expression didn't change. Mr McPherson glanced up before looking down at the hole.

"I wonder where that came from," he said, picking the ball out.

He looked at Sam. Sam shrugged.

Porteous then set himself up for the crucial putt. He was about to take a careful backswing when Mr McPherson said, "This ball looks very like the one his Lordship was playing earlier."

Porteous's demeanour instantly changed. He looked flustered, though he didn't look up. He stood over the putt. The crowd again quietened. Porteous stabbed at his shot and it shot forward, not only missing the hole but slipping well past, leaving him with a two-foot uphill putt.

"Ooohh," said the crowd

With his composure now gone Porteous's face reddened. He smacked the ground with his club. The Cleek's beechwood head flew off and skittered across the putting area. The crowd cheered and laughed.

"Borrow mine," said Elphinstone calmly.

Porteous took it without a word. He took a deep breath and steadied himself for the putt he needed to tie the match. But along with his composure had gone his co-ordination. His putt crept forward but drifted to the right and stopped half an inch from the hole.

The crowd cheered. Mr McPherson shook hands with both players. His Lordship smiled. Porteous stomped off and the crowd parted like the Red Sea to let him through.

Back at Straiton's Inn Sam didn't bother going to the after-match celebrations. He put the clubs in the clubroom and decided not to bother approaching Porteous for the usual caddie's tip, but instead helped himself to a piece of silver from the Ensign's cloak hanging on a peg.

He stood on a stool, climbed out a window at the rear of the inn, and made himself scarce.

Historical Note

This match was the first golf match ever reported in a newspaper – "a solemn golf match" was reported in 1724 in the Caledonian Mercury. There is no record of who won.

John Porteous was famously lynched by an Edinburgh mob twelve years later. As now Captain and leader of the town guard he ordered his troops to fire on a mob of demonstrators. For this the authorities imprisoned him. But, fearing the magistrates may pardon him, a mob broke into the jail, dragged him out and lynched him from a lamppost in Edinburgh's Grassmarket.

Lord Elphinstone fought a duel on Leith Links in 1729.

Leith Links players made the first ever written rules of golf in 1744. It's thought golf may have flourished in Leith due to local knowledge. Ship's carpenters had the skills to shape wooden heads and make a spliced joint to attach them while fishermen's tarred twine was used for whipping early clubs. The early clubs were the Longnose, Spoon, Niblick and Cleek, which used various types of wood.

The Citadel was a large defensive bastion. Built during Cromwell's occupation from 1650 to 1660, it covered a large area now occupied by Dock Street, Coburg Street, Cooper Street and part of Commercial Street. Remains of one gate can still be seen in Dock Street.

Straitons and Cants Ordinary were inns that stood in the Kirkgate for centuries. The latter was demolished in 1888.

Chapter 13

The Races

Water Street, Leith – 21st June 1746

Lillian sat at the dressing table, a frown on her elfin features. She loosened her light pastel blue gown; uncomfortable with that tight bodice, the fussy satin bows irritating. Her mother had followed her upstairs. There was a swish of skirts as she stepped into the room without knocking. Lillian glanced up but ignored the discontented expression on her mother's plump, wrinkled, over-powdered face.

"Before you ask," Lillian held up a palm towards her, "I will not marry Earnest Neil."

"And why not?"

Lillian was used to that edge to Mother's voice.

"Because he is old, and he is fat and ugly. He may be rich and Father may owe him money, but I don't care."

Earlier that evening, her parent's friends had all been there in the parlour of her father's large four-story house. Lillian hated them, and it took her best efforts not to show it. The Johnstons, the Dawsons, the gross fat Thompsons, and the crusty old Crawfords. And by far the worst, that pompous lawyer Earnest Neil with his sagging jowls and overpowering stink of hair oil.

The conversation was wide ranging though a good part of it was dominated by Mr Neil and her father droning on about the problems in the

Highlands and the sense of relief that the usurper Charles Stewart had at last been defeated at Culloden in April.

Earlier saw a fine spread in the dining room; duck, venison, mutton, pigeon, artichokes, French beans and cabbage and even these new vegetables now becoming popular. Lilian was not convinced she liked potatoes. Despite these distractions, she knew what this event was really about; she could tell from the glances, looks, and asides as the tiresome evening wore on. Glad when it at last ended and they said their goodbyes, Lillian stomped off to her room, leaving only her parents and Mr Neil in the parlour.

This kind of upset was a recent problem. It used to be her cosseted life was simple but now it all seemed so complicated. From the moment she had set eyes on Adam Preston, everything changed. At seventeen and with no previous experience in such matters, she struggled to understand these feelings coursing through her.

"Your father and I are not asking you to marry him today," said her mother, moving around the room and picking up a pair of gloves and a bonnet Lillian had discarded on the floor. "Mr Neil is taking us to the Leith races tomorrow, and has the best seats. It will be such fun! Talk to him at least."

For the last two months Lillian had spent most waking hours thinking of Adam. Her spirit rose at the thought of his wry smile and bright blue eyes. They had now met twice at the social evenings arranged by her cousin; they had kissed at the last. Lillian's third floor room was furnished well, with linen drapes, a comfortable feather bed and even the luxury of the finest mahogany chest for her large collection of dresses. However, it was also the scene of many arguments with her mother over the last few weeks. Lillian was a woman now; she had led a sheltered life, but knew she was attractive, and lively, and popular with others her own age.

"Mother," she said a bit louder than she intended, "I am not a little girl. I have reached an age where I will make some of my own decisions. You can't be telling me what to do all the time."

Lillian spent hours reading Romeo and Juliet and Anthony and Cleopatra. She had scoured the family library for romantic poems. She understood what love was, could feel it inside her, was adamant she would marry a man for love and not because it suited her parents.

"And what's the point," said Lillian, her voice rising. "If I talk to him, he will be encouraged and be even more annoyed when he discovers I won't marry him."

"You can still be courteous to him, that's what young ladies with your breeding do."

"Well I won't."

Her mother took a deep breath as she pulled Lillian around to face her.

"Honour thy father and mother," she said with a hiss. "So says it in the bible, and you," she pointed fiercely, "will do what your parents tell you."

She turned away dramatically, putting her hand to her brow. "Why, oh why are you so difficult and rebellious? I despair of you."

"I'm sorry Mother," said Lillian tersely.

Her mother pulled her from her seat. "Now go speak to him, he is downstairs. Tidy your dress, it's creased, see the satin and lace bows, straighten them up." She was fussing all over her.

Lillian's defiance returned. "The dress is fine," she said, irritated as she stomped out of the room and down the stairs. Her mother chased after her.

In the hallway, Earnest Neil stood before them, dressed in the finest quality of cloth. Lillian stifled a grimace at the sight of his bulbous nose, flabby lips and his usually thin hair plastered thickly to his skull. *Was that a wig?* she thought as he gave a low bow.

"Miss Lillian," he said ingratiatingly.

"Show Mr Neil our library," said her mother. "I'm sure he'd be interested."

"He wouldn't be interested."

"Lillian," said her mother a little too sharply.

"I'd love to see your library," said Mr Neil, bowing again.

Lillian shrugged huffily. "Follow me." She opened a door from the hallway and strode in.

Neil followed and picked up a book of love poems, flicked the pages and read, "The love of a good woman." He leered at her but quickly corrected himself when she frowned. "I'll be frank with you, Ms Lillian and not beat about the bush," he said becoming serious. "I have admired you from afar for many months and propose that you become my wife. As you are aware, I am a close associate of your father and he and I, we have come to an arrangement."

Lillian's gut lurched.

"As a wealthy man, I can offer you a life of luxury," he said moving closer. "My company has investments all over town; not only am I the finest lawyer in Leith but I have a stake in several shipyards." He started to count them off on his fingers. "Beatties, Davies and Todd's to name but three. The new glassworks that have recently opened on Baltic Street, I own twenty percent."

Neil then took from his pocket a small bag. Lillian's eyes widened as from it he pulled out a huge blue sapphire. He held it up and it glinted in the light; never before had she seen anything so beautiful.

"My deceased brother gave me this and for that reason it's my most precious possession, I keep it with me always." He looked at it lovingly. "I will make one exception; I will give this to the woman I marry."

For a few seconds Lillian was mesmerised, but then with a glance at his wizened face with a whiff of his foul breath, she almost gagged.

"But, in return," Neil leered at her through his yellow teeth.

"No," said Lillian.

Neil looked baffled. "But see what I offer you. If you are my wife people will respect you; you wouldn't have to involve yourself in anything other than keeping my house in order." His eyes narrowed, and he leaned closer. "Your father and I are in agreement, and I need a woman to serve my needs and bear my children."

Lillian looked horrified. "Then you should marry a girl who wants to have these things," she said, her voice sharp.

"But don't you?"

"I'm sure you could make a girl happy with your jewels and property but I want to marry for love and not to a man who wants a wife to be a servant."

Neil's expression changed. With anger in his eyes, he grabbed her arm. "What a feisty young filly, I like that," he said with a leering grin. "But your parents and I believe that some girls need a firm hand." He gripped her by both shoulders and tried to kiss her. Lillian's panic rose. She shook herself free and slapped him hard across the face.

"Mr Neil, you take liberties."

The lawyer reeled back in shock. She ran to the door but her mother burst into the room. It was obvious she had been listening outside.

"I won't marry a brute like him," said Lillian fiercely, pointing at Neil.

"Idiotic child!" screamed her mother, fury in her eyes.

Lillian steeled herself; she must not show weakness.

She turned to the lawyer. "But surely you don't want an unwilling bride."

"Now listen to me young lady," interjected her mother. "Mr Neil and your father have an arrangement, we have discussed it and the decision is made, you will marry Mr Neil."

Lillian turned fiercely, fists clenched. "I will not. I'm going to marry Adam Preston," she blurted.

Her mother and Neil reeled back.

"And who on earth is Adam Preston?"

"I have met him twice at cousin Stephen's social events, we have even kissed and I love him."

Her mother looked stunned. "Is it that boy I saw you with when I came to collect you from the dance last week?"

"Yes, I love him."

"Don't be ridiculous, we know nothing about him," hissed her mother.

The door swung open and her father stepped in, his, broad shoulders filling the doorway, a ferocious glare on his sagging face, though he spoke calmly.

"Apologies, Mr Neil for my daughter's behaviour. We will meet as planned at the races tomorrow where we shall be happy to accompany you to your grandstand seats. I'm sure we can have a fine day and we can use the occasion to announce your engagement." He motioned towards the door. "Now my dear," he mumbled to his wife, "if you could please see Mr Neil out."

Once they had left and the door closed, leaving the two of them alone, her father turned and backed Lillian into the corner.

"You," he said with an aggressive stare, "will marry whoever I choose."

Lillian trembled. She realised that she had gone too far. "I don't want an arranged marriage," she said meekly.

"You, young lady, will do what I tell you."

Lillian was aware that her father's debts were behind this; his poor investments had lost much of the family's fortune. He was in trouble. Her defiance returned.

"You only want to clear your debts," she shouted. "It's your own fault." Her tears welled up. "Why should I be unhappy because of you?" Her voice trailed off to a whimper. Her outburst had hit its target.

"You have a duty to the family."

His voice was cold as he took off his belt.

*

When Lillian woke the next morning, she gingerly touched the red marks on her painful thighs. Her emotions were shredded. Despite what had happened she was now even more determined; she would never marry Earnest Neil. At least she had learned the futility of trying to argue with her parents.

Mother was right about one thing, she really knew nothing about Adam – they had met at the dance, she didn't have any idea where he lived, who his family was or what he did. But she believed that it had been love at first sight for him as much as it had for her, she just sensed it. If only she could meet him again, but how?

Apart from their two meetings the only time she had spotted him was in the Kirkgate when she was out shopping with her mother. He passed by with two other young men; she only glanced at them for a moment but they looked a rough sort, not the type that someone like Adam would mix with. It must have been his employees, helping with whatever it was he did.

That morning Mother had insisted that new lace was added to the dress she was to wear to the races, With the great and good from Edinburgh and beyond attending, it was important the family made an impression.

At the Shore crowds were gathering. While the main action was down on the sands, the taverns did a roaring trade. Hawkers crowded the Shore along with added stalls selling everything from hot cakes to oysters to old shoes, supplementing the established booths and shops. Her mother dragged her to the haberdasher's shop having decided exactly what lace best offset Lillian's gown with its patterned silk and petticoats.

Lillian had shown little enthusiasm. In an attempt to placate her after last evening's events her mother had insisted on buying her an expensive new silver necklace from a stall by the Kings Wark. A purchase that would normally have excited Lillian but today she had little interest. When they arrived at the Haberdashers shop her mother at once went inside and started bartering with the shopkeeper.

Lillian stood at the doorway. It was a pleasant enough day, cloudy, perhaps with a hint of rain but only a light wind. Porters and carters were unloading a big old Galleon in from Holland. There was the whiff of tar and paint. A crane powered by a man walking a treadmill within its frame lifted barrels of wine from the hold and swung them onto the wharf. A relay of pairs of men hoisted and attached each barrel on their pole and carried it to the vaults.

Nails were being hammered on the far side of the water. In two places a deep channel had been dug into the bank and wooden walls added which jutted from either side into the river. In the first a sleek schooner was near complete, the other held the frame and keel for a Frigate. Dozens of men swarmed, sawing and hammering.

Then Lillian's heart missed a beat. There he was, Adam, strolling towards them along the quayside looking as if he had not a worry in the world. He swung a gold watch on a chain, and she sighed as she drank in his handsome good looks. She glanced into the shop; her mother resembled a dog after a bone when it came to haggling. She could spend all day if necessary, to get the best price. The shopkeeper was raising his eyes in exasperation as her mother gesticulated; he was in for a hard battle. That would keep her occupied for the next five minutes at least. Lillian took her chance and walked to the centre of the quayside and stood in Adam's path so he bumped straight into her. Their eyes met; Lillian's spirits soared. She was desperate to embrace him but knew she couldn't.

Adam smiled. "Lillian, oh Lillian."

She looked into his piercing blue eyes and shivered at the immediate connection between them. The words poured out of her like a tap while their eyes remained locked, never moving. It became a torrent, Lilian told him everything. Of her parents' attempts to arrange her marriage, of Earnest Neil and how much she detested him, of her father's beating, attending the races, the jewel.

And then she said, "I love you Adam, I want to run away with you."

Her heart sang as he smiled.

"Yes, oh yes." He took her hands in his.

Lillian's mother had made her bargain and was coming back out.

"I'll try to meet you at the races, look out for me," he said quickly, "and then tonight, come to the alley behind your house in Water Street, if you can. Creep out at ten."

Lillian's whole body shuddered as he kissed her.

"Our love will find a way," he whispered before making an exit just in time before her mother returned. Even the pain of her beating seemed to vanish as her mood soared.

For the races her mother insisted Lillian wore a red open fronted silk gown with cream petticoats over a tight white bodice with wide, turned back cuffs, on her head a straw hat with red ribbon. The family left Water Street in procession, her father at their head. On the beach the race meeting was in full swing when they arrived and they had to fight their way through the throng to the grandstand.

After the cloudy start it had turned out a lovely day with a light breeze. The Firth was quiet. Horses thundered along the sands cheered on by the huge crowd. There were stalls and booths with entertainments. All kinds of curiosities, strolling players performing on a makeshift stage, games of chance and skill, wrestling and cock throwing. The smell of roast pork, seaweed and ale. Rich mingled with poor and although it was only afternoon the mob were already rowdy; there had been one fight and by tonight no one would be surprised if there were more.

Neil and many of his guests were already the worse for wear when the family arrived at the enclosure. Lillian's father soon joined them. The temporary grandstand was erected in the best location. Lords and ladies, magistrates and judges all dressed in their finery juggled for space. Earnest Neil welcomed them and they joined the rest of his entourage in reserved seats They dined on oysters and beef while wine and spirits flowed in what was a boisterous occasion.

Lillian sat looking disconsolate, a frown on her face as she shuffled gingerly in her seat, still smarting from the bruising on her legs. Occasionally Earnest Neil would stagger up to her like some ugly strutting peacock to make a lewd remark and leer at her. Lillian ignored him and scanned the crowd for a sight of Adam.

Then she saw him from her vantage point, standing not one hundred feet away. She stood up and pushed past her parents and made a line straight for him. Her mother called after her. Lillian looked back but her mother was swamped by the crowd now on their feet as a large grey came thundering victorious to the finish line. Lillian ran out onto the sands.

"Adam, Adam," she shouted as she approached him.

He turned. "Lillian," he smiled.

Their hands came together; she was overwhelmed as they embraced. She held him tight. Moments later the angry figure of Earnest Neil forced himself between them, his face beetroot and angry. Lillian could see her parents coming down the stairs behind.

"How dare you sir," cried Neil, unsteady on his feet. Lillian could smell the alcohol on his breath.

Adam looked shocked and afraid but then he surprised her when, rather than run when he had the chance, he grabbed Neil by the lapels and grappled in a brief clinch as they swung unsteadily together. They stumbled then Adam pushed him and Neil fell backwards onto the sand where he floundered like a beached whale.

Adam turned and whispered, "Tonight, at ten."

He vanished into the crowd just as her parents arrived. As they helped Neil to his feet, his wig slipped off. Lillian couldn't help but giggle.

*

That night Lillian kissed her mother's forehead.

"Goodnight Mother, goodnight Father."

Rather than go up to her room she sneaked downstairs, crept through the kitchens to the back-stair's corridor, quietly unlocked the door and slunk into the garden. She recognised Adam's silhouette in the moonlight and ran to him. He cradled her face for a long, lingering kiss. Her knees weakened.

"Oh, Adam let's run away, we will have no money but take me away from all this."

"Money…"

He shook his pocket, a jangle of coin. Then took a small purse from his pocket, out of which dropped a large sapphire.

"Oh," said Lillian.

The creak of a door opening came from inside.

"Lillian, Lillian," called her father's voice.

Adam kissed her again. "There's been a change of plan."

Lillian's jaw dropped. "But when can we elope?" she squeaked.

In a flash he had slipped over the wall. Lillian's hand went to her throat, surprised to notice she had lost her new silver necklace. She jerked as Adam's head popped back above the wall.

"Sorry Lillian, but thanks for everything." He winked, and was gone.

*

Adam headed for home through the still raucous streets. Barbers, candlemakers and apothecaries had provided a lamp outside their premises which threw a glimmer of light on the thinning crowds as they drunkenly made their way back up towards Edinburgh. Adam fingered his pockets heavy with cash and jewels as he slipped into the darkness of the Yardhead slums.

Love the Leith races, he thought, *nice work when you can get it; wonder how much my old dad Sam lifted today? I bet my old grandad will be turning in his grave given he was once in the Leith town guard.*

He yawned as he reached his front door. Inside there was a nice fire going. He kissed his wife and knelt and hugged Ralph the baby and his two lovely daughters.

Historical Note

From at least the early 1500s until 1816, Leith Races were held each year on Leith Sands, an area north of the present Links and now built over. They were long regarded as one of Scotland's most important horse race meetings before racing moved to Musselburgh.

Chapter 14

The Highlanders

The Shore, Leith – 23rd April 1779

A smile creased Ralph Preston's weather-beaten face as he slipped his squat frame over the side. He landed softly on the deck of *The Trial.* It'd soon be dawn, quiet, the air still, was going to be a warm one.

This had been the risky part. He wiped the sweat from his brow and waited for his partner in crime. Thompson, the boatswain's mate landed beside him from following up the rope from the Jollyboat. On the south side of the river he could see the big crates of bottles in the gloom, a large stack piled outside the Old Ship Tavern. Behind them they had discreetly placed the barrels; no one would notice them among all the others.

They gave the thumbs up before moving down the ladder into the bowels of the brig. Relief coursed through Ralphs's body; they had done it. Under the cover of darkness, they had slipped six barrels of the best quality rum off the ship, six barrels in which they had invested in Jamaica and secretly carried with the other cargo from halfway around the world.

As the sun rose and the port came to life, Ralph relaxed in the wheelhouse with a mug of stewed tea, a smile on his plump, cheerful face. What might it mean? He could make Morag and wee Alexander happy. They might even move to a better house than the single room in that rickety, rat-infested tenement in Water Street.

*

"This is a farce." Captain McGraw's strong Hebridean accent boomed from the bridge, his giant muscular frame trembling with rage. "You can't move in this bloody harbour it's so crowded."

As his first mate Ralph knew from the thunderous look on his grizzled old face that it was best to keep his head down and avoid doing anything to annoy the big man when in this mood.

"At the double, Mr Preston, untangle her and let's get over the other side. Once this lot's unloaded, we pick up our next cargo, a human one this time. After that you can think about your shore leave."

Ralph touched his cap. Two days before they had arrived from the Caribbean in their big 333-ton twin masted brig. Since then they'd had to wait on the North Leith side of the river in the queue to unload on the Shore. Captain McGraw had heard they'd finally been allocated a space.

"Stand by to cast off, look lively you idle buggers," shouted the Captain.

Ralph ordered the crew to set a single jib to the fore of the two square-rigged masts. Curses and shouts came and then the squeal of halliards in blocks as they extricated themselves from the tangle of ropes and cordage belonging to the smaller smack next to them. The old brig creaked as they started to crawl away from their berth. They crept to the middle of the river at its mouth where a flood tide would help take them upstream. Ralph pushed the rudder away from him and they eased forward. On their left the Timberbush, a collection of workshops and warehouses. A high-pitched screech came from the marble polishing yard and the hint of the smell of tobacco from a big warehouse, though this was barely discernible among the overpowering stench from the whale blubber boiling sheds.

Ralph had rarely felt so good. A wide smile crossed his full lips. Today he was to go on leave after almost a year at sea and he also knew his life was to change. Their night time antics had enabled them to avoid the customs men.

When he left the vessel this afternoon, he would pick up his barrels. His old dad Adam would take them off his hands and move them on; he'd always been a right old crook (and womaniser), part of the local criminal fraternity. Ralph's profit on the venture would be over five times the wages he had earned as first mate on this voyage.

On both sides of the water, vessels lay alongside each other four deep, a mixture of large brigs, and the nimbler smacks half the size. They slipped passed a huge seventy-four-gun ship of the line which dwarfed the others, the Shore teeming as they approached. Stevedores, porters, sailors, and checkers fought with one another for space, cargo being carried across several decks before reaching the quayside and the same for everything being exported the other way. There appeared little rhyme or reason, proceedings looking more like a melee than what Ralph knew was, in reality an intricately coordinated system among the cargo handlers. Two cranes creaked and whined in protest as they groaned under the strain of their continual use.

The sounds of industry were all around. A dull thump came from the huge lead works in Constitution Street while sitting on the quay were several stacks of Leith pattern bottles, only a few of the million that were produced in the town every week. A heat haze shimmered above the rooftops on the quay from the direction of the glasswork's cones that towered above Salamander Street. Huge piled sacks of sugar waited to move to the old sugar house at the top of Tolbooth Wynd.

They arrived at their berth; the crew jumped ashore and secured the lines to the mooring rings. On the captain's signal the deck covers opened and the work of unloading began. The ship's men along with a team of local porters descended into the hold.

The afternoon was not a happy one for Captain McGraw. Their hold packed with rum, muscovado sugar, rice, indigo, mahogany and sago powder soon spilled out onto the wharf. The port customs officials stood like vultures, counting what came ashore and calculating the taxes due. Ralph couldn't help but smile as he observed the old captain become more and more enraged as the day went on and the bill mounted.

He had little sympathy for the grizzled old captain and watched with amusement as he spent much of the day gesticulating, raging and fuming. He appeared to be having argument after argument with the port checkers and customs men; as far as Ralph could see he was losing everyone. By the time the hold emptied he was in the foulest mood Ralph had seen for weeks.

For Ralph it was just the opposite. A thin smile crossed his face each time he checked his six barrels remained undisturbed, hidden behind the stock of bottles. Five hours later the work was near complete. As the light started to fade a rope on the hoist broke and the last sacks of rice needed to be relayed up by hand. Ralph climbed down the ladder to join the line until the hold was cleared, then clambered back up on deck, glanced up at the quay and almost fell over with shock.

The stack of bottles in front of the Old Ship Inn had gone and his six precious barrels now stood in the open for all to see. To his absolute amazement a troop of seventy tough looking Highlanders were lounging over them. They stood out in their smart red jackets and kilts, a burst of colour among the greys and browns of the buildings behind them.

"All right, Mr Preston lets be quick about it," bellowed Captain McGraw

"We only have a short time to bring the soldiers aboard – only then can you start your shore leave." His manner gruff, it was best not to argue with the mood he was in. "I'll be below."

Ralph took a deep breath to calm himself. He slowly recovered from the shock and waved to the soldiers to embark. Minutes passed. They made no sign of moving and continued to sit on their baggage and his barrels smoking and muttering. Something wasn't right. There was little speech among the men; they looked disconsolate sitting on their packs. He waved again, no response.

He made his way onto the quay and crossed the cobbles to talk to them. Again, he discreetly checked there was no problem with the rum upon which the Highlanders now sprawled. It was evident the men were disgruntled. Ralph was wary, they looked as tough as old boots and made a formidable sight in their kilts and uniforms and from what he had gathered they were renowned as fierce fighters. Ralphs's attempted to use hand signals to explain the need for them to come on board but that met with an angry torrent in an incomprehensible language from their sergeant.

Captain McGraw appeared on the bridge. "Mr Preston can you please explain to me why these fellows are not on the ship?"

Ralph sensed his anger simmering just under the surface.

"I don't know sir," Ralph shouted from the quayside. "There appears to be a kind of grievance but they are speaking another language – I've not a clue what they are on about."

The captain then strode down the gangplank and launched into an exchange with the sergeant in Gaelic as the officer gesticulated wildly throughout their brief discussion.

The Harbourmaster appeared, draped in a grubby black cloak, a heavy disgruntled man who gave an impression of having the weight of the world on his shoulders.

"I'm Ferguson, the Harbourmaster; what the hell is going on," he snapped. "Don't you understand that you should be casting off in five minutes?"

"It appears we have a problem," said McGraw lightly. "These men are from Lord Lovat's Highland regiment and appear to believe that if they accompany us, they will be forced to join a lowland regiment and that they won't be able to wear their kilts in the future – and I think it's safe to say they're not too happy about it."

Ferguson threw his hands up in exasperation. "What in the name of God has that to do with me? I've a harbour to run, you can see how busy we are."

After a further period of shouting, pointing and waving of arms it was obvious no progress was being made and with a look of irritation the Harbourmaster ordered one of his assistants to take a message up to the castle in Edinburgh.

Ralph's nerves were on edge – until they resolved this he couldn't leave. He was desperate to get home. He was very aware that Ferguson was within a few feet of his smuggled barrels; not a good scenario. What if he noticed them and became suspicious? Ralph felt helpless, the tension in his body causing a prickle of sweat on the back of his neck.

The hours ticked past and the standoff continued. There was a knock-on effect on the rest of the harbour, nothing moved. Ralph thought whether to ask the captain if he could start his leave but his expression told him the likely answer. McGraw had made one further attempt to reason with the soldiers but to no avail.

The thump of boots on cobbles suddenly broke the quiet. A unit of red-coated troops came marching in quick time from Tolbooth Wynd, halting in good order. At the rear was a tall officer on horseback. There was the clank of metal as a few Highlanders stood up and fixed their bayonets. Ralph's muscles twitched at the sound and he scampered back up the gangplank to the ship. The arrival of two hundred soldiers brought out crowds of locals spilling onto the quay eager to see what the excitement was about. The officer moved to the front of the column.

"Major Sir James Johnston, Commander of the South Fencibles," he announced. "Please step aside."

The captain cowered and ran up the gangplank and joined Ralph on the bridge. Ferguson and his assistants backed away. The Major was tall and lean, on his thin mouth an upper-class sneer.

"We have come to arrest these men." He snapped an order, and the Fencibles fanned out into line and surrounded the Highlanders. In response their anger increased. They grouped together, each with a musket or sword in hand.

There was a standoff, nobody spoke.

"Tell these fellows they are under arrest, and to set down their weapons," said the Major quietly

A sergeant from the Fencibles stepped forward and repeated the order in Gaelic, met with hoots of protest from Lovat's Highlanders, shouts and fists raised.

"I command you in the name of the King to lay down your arms," shouted the Major, standing up in his stirrups.

The Highlanders didn't move, but stood defiantly with their backs to the buildings.

"Recover arms!" screamed the Major.

In one fluid movement the front line of a hundred Fencibles knelt and lifted their muskets up to the firing position. The second line standing behind also brought their arms to bear. Suddenly a young Highlander broke from the group and ran for the end of the Fencibles line. A bearded corporal stepped forward to stop him. The young man raised his bayonet. The corporal started to draw his sword then screamed as the Highlander ran him through the chest. Smoke billowed as a musket fired from the Lovat line and another Fencible fell, his bloodied fingers clutching his gut, his scream that of a wild animal.

Half a second later there was a great flash as the front row of Fencible muskets fired in unison. Ralph ducked in panic. Smoke and the powerful smell of gunpowder came billowing over the ship.

Ralph peered back over the side, horrified. The second rank fired a volley. Screams and shouts filled the air as the surrounding crowd panicked, desperate cries from those trampled in the effort to escape the mayhem.

"Charge!" screamed Major Johnstone above the noise.

The Fencibles charged forward with yells and shouts, the ring of metal on metal as the two sides clashed in a scrum of hand to hand fighting. Ralph ducked again as the battle raged. After a minute the uproar subsided.

Ralph and Captain McGraw peeked over the gunwale.

The Shore lay thick with dead and groaning wounded, a few Highlanders still struggling with Fencibles who had wrestled them to the ground. Ralph shuddered as he surveyed the bloody scene.

The smoke began to clear.

He could hear the sound of liquid spurting and stared white-faced as the rum poured out of the dozens of bullet holes in his six barrels.

He looked at Captain McGraw whose face was drained and the colour of chalk. Their eyes met in the gloom and they together shook their heads in disbelief at what they had just witnessed.

"A terrible thing," whispered the Captain.

"A terrible, terrible thing," said Ralph as he watched his better life drain away across the cobbles.

Historical Note

Forty Highlanders of Lovat's Regiment and three of the South Fencibles died in this incident; the authorities were very keen to hush up the mutiny.

The Leith Glassworks stood on Baltic Street and dated from 1746. Leith specialised in wine bottles, largely for export to France and Spain. At its peak (c.1770) production was as high as one million bottles per week. The Leith pattern bottle is the parallel-sided, round shouldered, narrow neck bottle now dominant within the wine industry. Around 1770 the company branched into lead crystal glass under the new company name of Edinburgh Crystal.

Scotland's largest leadworks stood on the corner of Mitchell Street and Constitution Street. It was founded in 1760 and operational until the 1970s.

Chapter 15

The Fishwives

Newhaven – 23rd November 1812

Esmerelda Linton's heart missed a beat when she heard. Jimmy the tinker had come up in his cart from the port soon after dawn.

"The Ajax came in on the morning tide," he had told her.

Alexander had returned at last.

His ship was so late that it had haunted her he might never come back. Her belief he differed from most other men had begun to waiver; she wouldn't be the first woman to fall for a sailor and be abandoned with child.

Esmeralda could have found it awkward to find an excuse to leave the village but last night's northerly gale meant that none of the Newhaven boats had returned and had likely taken shelter on the Fife side of the Forth. The perfect reason to make her way along to Leith.

The storm had blown itself out though there was still a marked north wind. Small white clouds scudded over a blue sky above the Firth. At the little harbour she met with her friend Rose who lived on the opposite side of the tumbledown street of fisherman's cottages that made up the village of Newhaven. Into their creel baskets they put the accoutrements for the day. Gutting board and a sharp knife. Scales and paper for wrapping. They lifted them onto their backs and set off.

Rose was tall and slim, with wide laughing green eyes and an ample bosom. Esmerelda had the same attractive fair looks, smaller with a fuller figure, a snub nose with generous full lips. Esmerelda and Rose had sometimes been mistaken for sisters. They weren't, although through the close family links of Newhaven they shared four uncles, three aunts and nine cousins.

"So, Alexander's back," said Rose with a smirk.

"What's that to do with me?" said Esmerelda, a fierce glare in her bright blue eyes.

Rose laughed. "I know you're pregnant; the whole village does, it's no secret, you can even see it now."

Esmerelda walked on. Rose quickened her pace and caught up with her.

She grinned "Och, don't take it that way."

Esmerelda strode on, still frowning.

"And him not even a Newhaven lad; it's unusual. What does your father say? I'm surprised he allows it."

Esmeralda slowed, then allowed her puckered brow to turn to a smile.

"My ma and da they don't mind, there's advantages in having a sailor in the family given what they can smuggle. Anyway, whether it's a Newhaven man or a Leith man, they are all the same where it matters."

The girls glanced at each other and giggled. Esmerelda had had her eye on Alexander Preston for much longer than anyone else realised. When she first saw him, she knew that he was the man for her, with his lovely smile and expressive grey eyes.

"What was he doing before the whalers?" said Rose.

"He followed his old man out to the Caribbean when he was just a boy, thought he would try to smuggle rum like his dad had tried to, but ended up working on the slave ships, said it was awful work. Made him happy when he came home and got on the whalers."

The day he'd left six months before, what a day that had been. A blush flared on Esmerelda's cheeks at the thought. They had first made love in among the rocks by the beach. Afterwards she had joined the hundreds of others who had lined Leith pier with waving flags to cheer the whaling fleet as it departed the harbour.

"The thing about the whalers is that wages are good but there's no opportunity to spend money; perfect for saving enough for a marriage."

Rose and Esmerelda continued on the coastal path. A little spray broke over the rocks at the water's edge. A hundred yards offshore a handful of oyster boats combed the local beds.

They entered the town by Commercial Street and as usual they caused a slight stir with their traditional brightly coloured costumes. Cotton jackets with bright red and yellow mixed patterns, short woollen petticoats, the outer one kilted and with white worsted stockings and high shoes. They both wore a spotted cotton handkerchief around the throat and their rosy cheeked faces were topped with a cap with a lace border in the Dutch style. The stonemasons who were putting the finishing touches to the grand new Customs House by the bridge wolf-whistled as they passed.

They turned downriver. Just before the dry dock they stopped at the small wooden quay jutting from the bank where a little fishing skiff berthed. A tall young man was unloading his catch into large baskets and lifting them onto the rickety structure. He was working fast.

Esmerelda examined the ships that lined the Shore on the other side. There was a massive 74-gun ship in the line, preparing to leave.

Cries of "Hands aloft and loose the topsails!" and "Stand by to come about!" wafted across the water. These fighting ships were not such an uncommon sight over the past few years because of the war with Bonaparte. Its rigging was alive with sailors pulling on halliards and cords, there was the screech of ropes running through blocks as they raised a sail. Two large trading brigs were on the quay, both with their holds open. As usual the Shore was swarming with porters and stevedores lifting and carrying.

Esmerelda's heart lifted when she spotted the *Ajax*, lying in a berth further up, squeezed between two of the armed smacks belonging to the Edinburgh and Leith Shipping company. The whaling schooner was instantly recognisable with its row of harpoon irons on the bow rail.

"Hello Jaimie," said Rose, a coy smile on her lips.

The slim, muscular young fellow in the fishing skiff looked up.

"Why, it's the two most lovely girls in all Newhaven, what brings you here?"

"With the gale last night there's not a fish in the entire village so we thought we would try our luck with the most handsome fisherman in Leith," said Rose.

Esmerelda noted the twinkle in her eye.

"You in a hurry? You only just came in with your catch."

Jaimie glanced over the far side of the river.

"There's a press gang in town, wanting men for the navy, best not to hang around too long."

Rose smiled again. "Can we buy fish? We've not much money but we will help you with baiting your lines."

The deal was done and for the next hour they worked. Hundreds of hooks tied to the line, and each baited with mussels as they sang. Meanwhile Jaimie got the rest of his catch ashore and filled each of the girl's creels. When the two had finished baiting the last of the lines, they hoisted their laden baskets onto their backs.

"Goodbye Jaimie, and thanks, we are just goi—"

Suddenly they heard a piercing scream from the other side of the river, followed by loud shouts. Esmerelda looked across and scanned the Shore. Jaimie pointed at a commotion outside the Old Ship Tavern, two fellows being dragged out, one thrown to the road, the other jostled.

The press gang; you could tell from their sailor's jackets, the two struggling men being overpowered as the pressmen used their cudgels. Esmerelda's eyes widened; her jaw dropped. She recognised him at once. The man being manhandled was Alexander. She knew that body shape and his long wavy hair anywhere.

She stared white-faced, a wave of fear and helplessness coursing through her. *What could she do*? The man on the ground was being bound while two of the gang pushed and held Alexander against the front of the tavern.

Her muscles tensed as with a fast movement he suddenly shook himself free of his captors. He headbutted one and threw a punch at the other and was off in a flash. He swerved past a third and made a dash along the Shore towards the bridge. The press gang's officer shouted after him and led two of the pack in pursuit while the others struggled with the man down. Esmerelda felt her heart leap as Alexander jumped over packing cases and fish boxes, pushing them over behind him.

She dashed back along the bank and swung onto the bridge. Alexander careered onto the other end and tore towards her, followed closely by the three press gang men in hot pursuit.

A slow-moving cart was crossing, overloaded with great bales of hay. Alexander darted through the gap, a terrified look on his face. For a second he stumbled as he recognised her; she signalled him to keep running and he burst past at full speed.

Esmerelda stepped into the gap between the wagon and the wall as the press men were charging through from the other end. She stumbled and tripped, her whole basket of fish emptying into the path of the oncoming gang. The first two slipped and landed painfully on their backsides with a crash; the third, being unable to stop in time tumbled over them, sending the three sprawling.

The cart stopped. A confused mass of press gang men, fish and Esmerelda filled the gap. A dog sitting next to the wagon driver barked. The press men all swore; Esmerelda screamed. She glanced backwards to see Alexander dashing along the bank and then behind the buildings, vanishing from sight. The press men managed to stand up and dusted themselves down.

"This is an outrage," screeched Esmerelda. "Can honest folk not get on with their daily lives without being attacked by a bunch of vagabonds on the street? I've a good mind to call the magistrate – and look," she picked up a mackerel with one hand and threw it at them; with the other she grabbed a large haddock and slapped it across the face of the press man nearest to her, "all my fish, ruined."

The three looked startled. Faced with an angry Esmerelda they hesitated. Then pushed past her and continued their chase.

For the next half hour Esmerelda couldn't remember ever being so terrified. *What if they found him? What could she do but wait?* She could hear heavy footsteps on the cobbles as the press gang searched and researched the narrow lanes of North Leith, their eyes probing every possible hiding place

The girls returned to the little wooden wharf to replenish Esmerelda's basket from Jaimie's catch. He'd had the good sense to make himself scarce. Once filled they again pulled the heavy creels on their back; the press men were standing by the Customs House as they left. Esmerelda and Rose gave them their fiercest scowl but said nothing. They crossed the bridge and strode up the eastern road towards Edinburgh.

It was only when they got halfway up to the Abbey Hill that they felt it safe to stop. Esmerelda swung her heavy creel onto the ground. She removed a few fish from the top, put in her hand and pulled out a wet, fishy Alexander. He stood up and stretched his stiff limbs. He put his hand in his shirt and drew out a herring.

"Bugger this, I'm giving up the sea and going to find a job indoors on dry land," he said.

"You stink of fish," said Esmerelda.

"So do you," said Alexander, smiling.

Esmerelda smiled back, then he kissed her.

Historical Note

It's unclear when the women of Newhaven started selling fish in Edinburgh but it's thought to be from the early 1800s until the 1950s.

Oyster beds in the Forth had been famous for their abundance and quality until the mid-1800s. The greed of the Edinburgh authorities in charging increasing rents meant that in an attempt to be profitable the beds were overfished, stripped bare and destroyed.

Whaling from Leith started from 1615. It declined in the 1840s but in the first half of the 20th century the Christian Salvesen company restarted annual sailings with advanced factory ships. Overfishing again led to a decline and the last ship sailed in 1963.

Robert Reid built the Leith Custom house in Commercial Street between 1810-12. It was here that ship's skippers paid duties and declared their cargos.

Impressment by a press gang was a practice of forcefully taking men into the navy. The practice started in 1664 and fell into disuse after 1815 after the defeat of Napoleon.

In June 1811 a statistical population census gave the population of South Leith as 15,938; North Leith 4,875.

Chapter 16

The Bank

Leith Links -20th September 1842

Annette looked out over the Links. *So beautiful,* she thought, *just like her.*

"Quick, if you want a lift. I need to get to the bank," shouted Albert from the stables.

Annette skipped with grace down the steps of their substantial house. She smiled; the horse stopped. Albert bent forward from the front seat of the gig. Annette stretched upwards; their lips met for a lingering kiss.

"Lovely darling, drop me in town," she said in a soft voice and climbed up beside him. "I need to catch the coach to Edinburgh, lots more shopping to do."

Albert looked at her and beamed. He agreed with everybody else, Annette was the most beautiful young woman in Leith. How could anyone doubt it? It was not only her physical beauty that drew everyone to her, they also admired her kindness and gentleness.

Annette stood out. Most people agreed that she was a perfect example of womanhood. Her skin perfect, unblemished, white with a hint of colour. Her dark hair thick, luxuriant and attractively styled, her fine long fingers exquisitely manicured. She had perfect breasts, both pert and fulsome. She wore stylish clothes like today's beautiful purple bell-shaped dress, and while these often appeared to be modest, they were always adjusted with care to accentuate her curves.

The horse took the strain, and they set off down the drive. Today's destination brought back memories of her father; he had doted on her. When her mother died, she had taken her place on all social occasions and often accompanied him, be it socialising with his banker friends, (Leith being home to five competing banks) or with important merchants and industrialists in Leith and up in Edinburgh. Balls, dinner parties and dances became the norm. Annette had rarely been far from his side.

"And why don't you pop in and say hello to your sister Ella?" said Albert with a grin. "Ha, your ugly little sister." He slapped his thigh and laughed out loud at his own joke.

Before he died a few months previously, Annette's father Mr John Braithwaite had spent his working life making a success of the Leith Banking Company. He took great pride in the fact they issued their own banknotes. The fine premises in Bernard Street were part of his legacy. From humble beginnings he made his way to become the senior director and major shareholder. During all of this time his personal assistant Mr Alexander Preston had ably assisted him.

She frowned. It was a joke she had heard many times before.

"Really, Albert you must stop saying that about her, it's impolite and rude."

Annette thought of Albert as her reward for the many years she spent honing her skills. She worked hard to develop a bearing and posture which at the same time managed to appear both submissive and alluring; she had long realised that when added to her looks this seemed to make men want her. She still liked the stir she caused among them wherever she went.

"It's not her fault she looks the way she does."

A few weeks before her father died, she married Albert. As the eldest son of Lord Haddington, they had a sumptuous wedding with over 300 guests at the finest halls in Edinburgh. He was the perfect match. Handsome, charming, and not particularly clever – and he would also inherit a large estate and title near Tranent. Her only disappointment was that due to his father's mismanagement his family was penniless, even gambling away the compensation payments from the loss of their large holdings of slaves when abolished a few years ago. However, when she weighed it up, it was worth it for the title. The fact that when his father died, she became Lady Haddington warmed her heart.

They trundled down Elbe Street at a canter, the light wind ruffling her ringlets under a jaunty yellow bonnet.

"As for our trip next month," said Annette, "The question is whether we go to Paris, Vienna, Milan and Rome or Paris, Rome, Milan and Vienna."

"Mmm, we need to consider that," said Albert.

"That reminds me – I must ask old Preston about getting foreign currency."

Annette was excited that now a respectable period of mourning for her father had passed she could at last release the purse strings; it was time for her and Albert to step onto a bigger stage. She still missed her dear father and knew that Leith had provided the source of her fortune. However, it had become a centre for industry along with the dirt, grime and noise that that entailed, and she deserved more than a bustling port town offered.

Annette decided that a girl as bewitching as her deserved not only to be wealthy, but to be rich, really rich. To join the aristocracy; a fine estate with excellent hunting. A second house in London and a grand tour of Europe and maybe America. There was one way to go and that was up.

"Apparently your sister's now old Preston's new assistant, I'll never understand what your father was thinking of. Why did he leave your sister any of his money when to look at her it's clear she has not a clue how to spend it?" He tittered again and slapped his thigh.

They turned into Bernard Street. *Her sister*, thought Annette. In a strange way she missed her since she left her father's house when she got married. Her sister had been the only person in the world to whom she had ever been able to show the less sweet parts of her personality.

For Ella she had always had a sharp tongue when they were alone. Throughout their childhood she rarely missed an opportunity to put Ella down. Sometimes even in public (in the politest way of course and often disguised as praise). With her private teasing, taunting and ridiculing she had taken delight in pressing home any advantage. Even when well aware that her words hurt. From an early age she sensed that Ella was a rival for her father's affections, and there was only ever going to be one winner. Annette had always taken pleasure in piercing a dagger through Ella's heart. She had always enjoyed Ella's tears.

*

Mr Alexander Preston and Miss Ella Braithwaite made their way on foot along the Shore up towards the bank's chambers in Bernard Street. His early morning meeting was with a fish exporter in the docks but now Mr Preston was at a loss for words. He wasn't looking forward to the two meetings he needed to attend in the bank later that day.

Mr Preston was a rotund little man in late middle age. He sported a clipped moustache which seemed out of balance with his bushy eyebrows, had a florid complexion and walked in a quick, brisk manner. He wore a sombre dark suit and to people he didn't know he appeared as what he was, a banker. To see him today no one would have believed he was a sailor in his youth and worked on slave ships and whalers.

Mr Preston had to admit that he now saw this dumpy, podgy, spotty young woman by his side in a new light, but there was an awkwardness between them. Since their discussion three days ago there seemed little more to say.

He remembered her father once telling him that while she wasn't attractive, she had been the clever one. The tutors and governesses he employed reported that while Annette excelled in the arts and social graces Ella had shown an aptitude in all subjects, be it Latin or literature or maths and arithmetic. He could also recall him once admitting that while Annette filled his home with colour and vitality, Ella by comparison was so quiet you barely noticed her. He believed it strange the two sisters were so different; Annette so vivacious and Ella in the background, to the extent you sometimes didn't realise she was even there.

Mr Preston was acutely aware that the silence between them had become deafening

"I.. I can remember only twenty years ago I attended the public hanging of pirates on the Leith sands, near the bottom of Constitution Street. Incredible how things have changed over that time – I think that was the last remnant of how the world was in my father's and grandfather's day."

Ella acknowledged him with a nod and a smile from her narrow lips, so thin it barely creased her waxy skin.

He could remember he and his other banking colleagues always thought it strange when she first arrived. Most wealthy young women went straight into the marriage market; the only real option for an unmarried woman of gentle birth was to become a governess. It raised a few eyebrows when her father employed her at the bank. It was unusual for a young woman to enter the world of banking, though not unknown.

He observed that from her junior position she had, over time shown herself to have an aptitude for finance. She even grasped the more complex aspects of the organisation. Although quiet she was businesslike and effective and over a period of years, he learned to respect her decision-making skills and work ethic.

"I remember the pier being extended then, the first sign of the real growth to come. The changes have been thick and fast ever since; the march of new technology has led to a huge rise in demand for dock space. See how busy it is with the steamers lying four or five abreast."

Ella acknowledged with another nod and mirthless smile. Preston was relieved that conversation was now difficult thanks to the noise of the thumping pistons of a passenger ship from the London and Edinburgh Steam Packet Company as it started to chug away from the wharf. A filthy coal boat also prepared to leave, its boilers having built up the necessary head of steam. The thick fog from their funnels mixed with the damp haar drifting in from the sea; the smell of engine oil and grease gelled with the overpowering stink of boiling whale blubber from the yard at Timberbush.

Mr Preston had been an observer, and had watched the town go through astonishing changes during his thirty years at the bank. The past two decades brought a boom in industry. Mr Braithwaite's sound management along with wise investments in new technologies had, until the recent crash led to great rewards for both himself and his customers. As commerce grew so had the bank's profits.

Sail was giving way to steam – the first steam ship ever to cross the Atlantic, the "SS Sirus" was built at the Menzies shipyard by the East Dock gates only a few years before. Warehousing and pier facilities improved. Despite the recent slump there was now talk of further expansion of the East and West docks and even of further railway lines coming into the town.

The embarrassed silence continued; Preston was glad when they at last reached the bank and went straight up to her father's old office. Minutes later Albert and Annette were ushered in. The room was a grand affair. Big windows onto Bernard Street, tasteful decorations and furnishings and above the polished wooden floor a high ceiling with beautiful cornices.

Annette gave Preston her most brilliant smile. He looked at her longingly (he had enjoyed her from every angle in his many fantasies about her). Annette then did what she did for all men, the smile, lowering her long lashes and then raising them to offer a direct gaze from her gorgeous hazel eyes for just one and a half seconds too long, before lowering them again. Annette had always taken delight that this small act could lead to a man pursuing her, often to the point of making a complete fool of himself for many months and in one or two past cases, even years.

"If his Lordship could come and sign a few documents in the next room before our meeting," said Preston, "I'd be most grateful."

Preston and Albert moved next door leaving the two sisters alone. Ella sat and pushed a string of unruly hair into her bun.

Annette looked at Ella and smiled. "What lovely hair."

Ella shuffled the papers on her lap.

"And that dress, I owned one very like it back in '35, when it was in fashion; I loved it."

Ella kept her eyes on her documents.

"Surely it's a little too small for you."

Annette wandered round the room. She checked the mantelpiece for dust.

"I hear they have promoted you to Mr Preston's personal assistant. Well done you; Daddy would be so proud." She gave a mocking snort and moved closer.

"It's good for the likes of you to have a career; no one will ever want to marry such a tubby little thing."

Ella studied her papers.

"Oh well, if you don't fancy chatting, I might as well go," said Annette, her top lip raised to a sneer as she headed back to the door as the two men returned. "I'm sure we will meet again in another year."

Ella glanced up. "Time will tell, Annette," she whispered.

Annette gave Albert a peck on the cheek.

"See you tonight darling."

She moved close to Mr Preston, just to let him smell her before making her final farewells and fluttering out of the room.

Preston took a deep breath to compose himself. He decided that informal was best, so they sat in comfy chairs beside the small fire that he lit.

Alexander put on his brightest tone. "Ah it's an honour to do business with you again sir, take a seat."

Albert smiled warmly, his good looks and open face with the look of a puppy aware it was about to receive a titbit. Preston ordered Ella to pour the tea as he fussed around the young man.

"All right," said Albert, "let's not beat about the bush, let's get to business."

Mr Preston smiled his best smile, but then found the words he required wouldn't come. There was a silence. Ella handed round the cups. She had small, dark eyes which appeared a deep brown but when the light caught them, you saw they were actually green. She had a silent way of watching, as if she were a cat.

"What's the dividend this year; out with it man," said Albert.

Preston wriggled in his seat.

"What do you know about banking?" he said in a serious tone.

"Banking, nothing of course; that's your job old chap," replied Albert slapping his thigh once again at his joke.

Albert knew that now, due to his wife's assets, he was a wealthy man. It was only proper that as the man of the house he would take a lead role in overseeing their management. Yet what he didn't envisage was that it was ever something in which he would become personally involved; such things were looked after by servants and stewards, and by lawyers and managers. Their job was to ensure that the landowner's business was done and done well. It was clear to him that Mr Preston was in this category.

"What the bank tries to do is to provide the people who deposit with us with a satisfactory rate of interest on their investment." He took a sip of tea. "Your dividend, as you call it."

Preston shifted his position again.

"And yet the other side of the coin is that people who borrow from us want to for long periods at low rates."

He studied Albert closely for a sense of understanding. Ella sat watching, notebook in hand.

"So, you see there has to be constant compromise between the two, the depositors and borrowers."

He detected that Albert was confused.

"You see, the last few years haven't been so good as in the past, problems started a while back due to the banking crisis in '37. This year there have been some … mmmm... What should I call it…" He reached to take another sip of tea but then decided against it. "Complications."

"Complications?" said Albert.

"You see to be successful a bank has to provide savers and depositors such as yourself and your good lady wife with investments that can be converted into cash as required, but that offer a high yield of return. Yet borrowers expect us to lend them money for significant periods at low rates. However, at the same time they want us to accept that there may be a risk that they might default on their loan,"

He studied Albert again hoping to see a spark of understanding.

"We have to strike a balance you see, simply because there's great risks attached to financing long-term loans with short-term deposits."

"Look," said Albert his earlier smile now gone, "I've come here today to hear what the dividend on our investment has been for the year past. Ask me of hunting, gaming or running an estate and I can help you but I don't understand what you're talking about."

His exasperation was becoming clear. He looked at Preston, who kept his face expressionless. He glanced at Ella. Ella smiled and watched.

"I know nothing about banking, or commerce or quarrying or mining or shipbuilding for that matter. I wouldn't expect to know these things; that's your job."

They stared at each other in silence for what seemed to Alexander Preston to be long seconds.

"The dividend for the year is unfortunately zero," said Preston.

"Zero?" said Albert, his face reddening.

Mr Preston rose from his seat and moved to his desk. Albert looked at Ella with an expression of disbelief. Ella smiled, creasing the dark shadow on her upper lip.

She spoke, "And I'm sad to say it's not only that; unfortunately, the bank has also failed."

"Failed?" said Albert with a look of utter confusion.

Mr Preston lifted a small bell from his desk and rang it.

"When a bank fails, it can be a worrying thing," said Ella. "It's a concern that it may lead to a loss of confidence," she paused, "and a failed bank can be an unfortunate thing for some investors, depositors and shareholders."

Albert sat with a stunned expression and stared at her. Ella gave him her sweetest smile through her crooked teeth.

"You see," interjected Preston, "There have been several complications this year. The collapse of the cotton trade, a lack of engine boilers, an oversupply of coal and failed harvests on the continent."

Preston looked out the window, the dusty street below busy with carts and carriages.

"I'm afraid to say that what this means is that all your funds have gone. It's unfortunate that they had links to a few unlucky investments."

"Gone?" said Albert, "what do you mean, gone?" He jumped from his seat looking like he was about to explode. "Now you listen to me," he shouted.

A side door opened and two large uniformed security guards entered. They positioned themselves in front of Albert. Ella stood up, smiled at him and left the room.

"I'm very sorry but there's nothing I can do, and I am very busy," said Mr Preston matter-of-factly. He turned to the guards. "The young sir is just leaving, please see him out."

For his next meeting Mr Preston had undertaken hours upon hours of preparation. Over several days he worked far into the night and had left no page unturned. He read and reread everything in the bank's vaults and filing rooms, papers on every subject. He had gone through all their accounts and loans, studied relevant commercial law and read the bank's articles of association. He examined every legacy, every investment, and every trust fund. Eventually he had to admit defeat. Although it rankled, he also had to admit a grudging respect for the abilities of young Miss Braithwaite.

He recalled his own words of only a few days before even although he was alone in his office.

"My goodness me," he exclaimed to himself as he raised his eyes from the ledger, "she is a clever girl."

Their meeting lasted only a matter of minutes; such was his shame and embarrassment, and also, he realised he couldn't meet her eyes. There were no niceties as Ella got straight to business.

"Sign these," she said thrusting him a thick pile of parchments. "And all your little mmm … let me think, what will we call them," she mused as she put her podgy finger to her narrow lips, "errors, will be forgotten."

"Ah yes, Miss Braithwaite." He adjusted his tie and picked up the nib. "Most kind, Miss Braithwaite," he said in his most submissive tone.

Preston felt the spasm of shame as he realised how much he was grovelling. He still found it hard to fathom how this plain little young woman could have outmanoeuvred him so completely. With her bad skin and small dark eyes, she was so unlike her sister. It was difficult to believe they came from the same mother.

Once he signed Ella picked up the papers, then swept from the room without another word. Preston was left with his thoughts. He knew that now these papers were signed, that tiny mouse of a young woman was presently in control of the Leith Banking Company. That as of tomorrow she would become a significant shareholder in the much larger bank with which it was soon to merge. He knew that although the bank had failed, all its sound assets would transfer with her, but the toxic investments responsible for its demise would be left behind.

For Mr Preston there was no real choice. Both he and Ella were aware that his fraudulent activity she'd uncovered gave him little room for manoeuvre. If he followed her instructions, face could be saved and he would avoid scandal. It meant that he would escape going to prison and keep much of what he had skimmed off over the past decade. Mr Preston could still have a comfortable retirement; he would have stopped soon anyway. His new young wife and their little Isaac would be secure and he could golf on the links twice a week. He could have no complaints.

*

Late that afternoon Albert sat at home staring into the fire, his two large hounds at his side.

Annette entered the room with a huge bunch of flowers. There was a bustle of activity as she started to split and arrange them among three different vases.

"Have a good day at the bank, darling?"

"Not particularly," replied Albert. "There's a bit of a problem."

"A problem, what sort of problem?" she said as she decided the Begonias should go in the smaller vase.

"How can I put it? W … we… I… It's possible we will need to spend a little less in future."

Annette giggled. "Well funnily enough I was just thinking how as it's our first trip away we should do the grand tour of six European countries rather than the ten we had planned."

She finished the flowers and stood back to admire them.

“Look, I must rush; I’ve got to meet with the designers. Remember we have the theatre this evening then you can tell me all about it afterwards at dinner.”

She swept from the room. For once Albert didn’t notice how fantastic she looked. His head dropped and he held it in both hands. He covered his ears with his thumbs and eyes with his middle fingers as he felt tears well up. He let out a quiet sob. A dog looked up.

In the hallway Annette stopped by the full-length mirror at the bottom of the stairs to study her reflection. A small satisfied smile crossed her full rosebud lips.

Annette was beautiful.

“Yes, I am,” she said aloud.

Historical Note

The Leith Banking Company opened in 1793 and was forced to merge due to debt in 1842. Its premises still stand at 25 Bernard Street. The bank grew during a time of prosperity in the early 19th century following the development of the town's harbour, pier, warehousing and dock facilities. After the financial crisis of 1837 it began to struggle. It merged with others which eventually in turn merged with the Clydesdale Bank. It's reported that Sir Walter Scott held an account there.

Chapter 17

The Docks

The Docks, Leith -6th February 1882

A rare satisfied smile crossed the stern features of Archibald Currie.

With the new Edinburgh Dock now complete it could only get better. More dock space meant more capacity. More capacity meant more demand and of course, more demand meant more money. Looking out from his office window he realised he had achieved what he had set out to do.

In the new dock one of his ships was berthed. Hard to miss with his name emblazoned along the side. The docks were overflowing. Closest to him the sleek lines of a fine-looking Clipper, one of the fast sailing ships. They still had a part to play. But in contrast next to that, a huge navy warship with its great guns, one of the Ironclads. That was the future, iron and steam.

Here he was, in his late fifties. Yes, his hair was thinning and he could do with losing a few pounds at the waist. Despite that, he still had the vitality of his youth. He had tripled his fortune over the past few years and reached his goal of becoming one of the most important men in Leith. The company now owned and operated twenty-two steamers that traded goods all around the world.

Archibald glanced at the photo frame on his desk. He experienced a twinge of irritation. That niggling thought came into his mind; it didn't fit with his vision. He shook it away.

Archibald could see the future. He had plans. Grain ships, refrigeration ships, cattle ships, whale factory ships and cable-laying ships. The possibilities were endless. This he knew was all to come. Then there was the expanding railway network along with the many new industrial processes that were being introduced on a near-daily basis. Prospects looked bright.

He put on his bowler hat and lifted his coat.

Although cold it was a fine winter afternoon, and he thought to take a detour to the new developments in Henderson Street. The beginnings of a huge building site. Here the modern stone tenements would rise to replace the teeming slums of the Yardheads and St Anthony's. Eighteen ancient closes to be swept away in the improvement scheme.

How grand compared to things in his youth. Despite the success, he had not forgotten his roots in Leith. With business interests in textiles, esparto grass for paper, sugar refining and brewing, his tentacles now stretched into all parts of the town, while just last week he had taken a stake in Sanderson's whisky and Rose's lime juice.

He strolled back along Tolbooth Wynd to the beautiful ancient four-story house in Water Street. Following the death of his wife he now shared it with his three daughters, and his two spinster sisters.

Then, of course, there was Mathew, his only son. Exasperation rose in his gut once again. It was the only thing causing him dissatisfaction. Mathew, his sop of a son and now that new bride of his, that Mary Preston girl. Pretty enough but lacking a bit of decorum at times. Mathew had married beneath himself. He would have a word with him; she needed to be whipped into line.

*

Today Mary looked happy. She wore a simple white dress which seemed to fit with her large blue eyes. Small fair and lithe, her delicate features framed by expressive eyebrows, she had managed to find exactly the cabinet she wanted after months of looking. A rich dark mahogany, inlaid with intricate designs in mother-of-pearl. She knew at once it would fit perfectly under the window of their bedroom. The cabinetmaker had delivered it that afternoon, and she stood admiring it in the hallway.

By chance, Mathew and his father arrived home at exactly the same time. Mary could still be surprised by the difference between them when standing together. Archibald Currie was sixteen stone, tall and broad, balding on top but with bushy, greying whiskers. Mathew, by comparison, was lucky if he was nine stone. His slight frame looked like it was struggling to fill his fine tailored suit. But still so handsome in that boyish way that Mary liked. All three studied the cabinet.

"Charming, charming," said Archibald with a thin smile. "This is a lovely piece of furniture."

"Yes, I loved it as soon as I saw it," said Mary, with obvious enthusiasm.

Archibald put a finger to his chin. His smile faded. "However," he said with a look of slight consternation, "when I bought this house with my now dearly departed wife, we together furnished it in an adequate manner. It's in a particular style she favoured; I remember she gave it a great deal of thought."

Mary frowned. Mathew took a step back and started to fill his pipe. Archibald slowly stroked his whiskers.

"Now, if we add furniture of a different style, surely there's a danger that it might not fit in. The harmony of the space could be affected." He turned and looked at Mary. "Good friends of mine understand the importance of these kinds of things. They may think the worse of me."

Mary felt herself colour.

"We are putting it in our own room so only we will have to see it, aren't we Mathew?" said Mary, a little more sharply than she intended.

"I … eh…" stuttered Mathew.

"Surely you must understand that the disharmony could well spread into other rooms all around the house. Such a move would therefore be," Archibald's thin smile returned, "inappropriate."

Mathew, eyes down, continued fiddling with his pipe and tobacco.

"It's all about taste you see; I'll have the butler remove it to the servant's quarters." With that, he pivoted and walked into his study, closing the door behind him.

*

Although she had only been married six months Mary already knew her father-in-law better than most other people. She had studied him closely. She was well aware he made a formidable opponent.

At home he was master, and the same applied to all his many business interests. He was the master, but not in an arrogant way. It could take some time before you began to feel the crushing pressure of his authority. Even when he wasn't actually there Mary realised nobody was free of it. Everybody, his family, his staff, his servants spent most waking moments asking one question: What would Mr Archibald Currie think?

Mary had observed that of course he would never be seen to bully anyone. On the face of it he was far too polite, too considerate. And yet she was aware everyone found it impossible to relax in his presence. With him, you expected to be interrupted but never to interrupt. If he was reading you felt you had to keep quiet, though this would never be reciprocated. In his study, it was absolutely forbidden to disturb him without a specific invitation yet nowhere and no one was out of bounds for him. He always seemed to make a noise. Snapping his watch shut, swinging in his chair, tut-tutting, snuffling and loud breathing. Yet no one would consider doing such things in his presence. Everyone knew that if you gave your own views on any matter, he would immediately swamp you with his. Guaranteed to appear much more reasoned and better explained and with a bludgeoning wit.

Mary ran up the stairs to their room and slammed the door.

His family and servants also knew their world moved to his routine. The day would begin when he arrived in the parlour to lead prayers at 7 a.m. (woe betide any staff or family member who was ever late). Breakfast was at 7.10 prompt, and to finish no later than 7.35. He would go to his study and from then until 10.30 a.m. everyone was expected to be ready to see him if required. Then a brisk walk to his office at the docks. In the afternoons he would visit his many business interests. However at least once per week, he would reappear at home unexpectedly and so everyone was always on edge, waiting, just in case.

He would either go out to meetings or work in his study in the evenings. Final prayers were at 10.30 p.m. and the house had to have all lights extinguished by 11 p.m. at the latest.

Mary was also well aware that he totally dominated his son, her husband Mathew, along with the three daughters and two sisters who lived with them. Mathew was so kind and gentle and she loved him with all her heart. However, it had become clear to her he couldn't stand up to his father in any way whatsoever.

*

"Hello darling," said Mathew brightly.

Mary sat in front of the mirror fiddling with her hair, still fuming after the cabinet episode; that had been the final straw.

"Had a good day?"

Mary sat with lips sealed, struggling to control her anger. The silence stretched.

"Is anything the matter dear?"

She remained silent. The spark that lit the fuse was the condescending tone used when he said, "Now Mary, let's not be silly."

"Three guesses," she snarled.

"Darling, I know Father can be difficult at times but we have to remember that this is his house and I would rather not cause any unpleasantness."

Mathew came across and bent to kiss her

Mary twisted round and slapped him. He looked stunned, fear in his eyes.

"Why … what was that for?"

What do you think it was for?" she growled. "You took his side; you scurried back to Daddy."

Mathew looked angry. "Now look here," he said grabbing her tight by the arm. "No wife of mine is going to…"

Then all restraint was gone. Mary stood and bombarded him with her resentment and anger. She gesticulated wildly, and she screamed and shouted. She raised her fists and stabbed her finger, she surprised herself with the ferocity of her all-out attack. After five minutes she was spent, exhausted, her eyes ached, she felt tired and miserable. This filthy row had achieved nothing.

They slept in separate beds that night. She didn't go down to breakfast the next morning, and left the house early to spend the day with her own family at her father Isaac's house in Baltic Street. Normally she would have taken Mathew but not today; she was glad to have the excuse to visit as her older brother had a new set of twins, Frank and Tony.

The following day was Sunday. The usual routine was that the Currie family would meet in the hallway before walking in procession to the best of the private pews at South Leith Parish Church. Archibald would lead from the front.

Mary crept down the stairs; her luck was in. Mathew, prompt as always was alone in the hallway. She grabbed him by the arm and led him out the front door. Mathew looked nonplussed for a second but didn't resist.

"I'm sorry I lost my temper – we need to go for a walk."

"What are we going to…"

"Quiet," she said firmly and put her finger to her lips.

They said nothing as they walked down Broad Wynd and up along the Shore. It was cold enough for snow to threaten, a low bright sun reflected on the river. Two swans swam on the far side. Seagulls squabbled over scraps.

A throng of porters with trunks, merchants with their wares and passengers in travelling cloaks and wool hats, some smiling, others in tears, milled around the shore. A piercing whistle came from a passenger steamer of the Leith, Hull and Hamburg Steam Packet Company as it approached the quayside churning up the murky water, spouting thick steam. The smell of oil, rust and grease hung in the damp air. They crossed the bridge and past the Customs House before heading towards Newhaven. A hundred yards along the road they turned off and a little further on stood in front of a little cottage on the outskirts of town.

"It's not working Mathew."

Mathew said nothing.

"I remember when you used to paint, and sing and read poetry, now all you do is work."

She grabbed his arm.

"Well yes … eh … but Fathe…"

"I want us to move to our own house."

"B … but."

"Look at this beautiful little house; it will suit us perfectly. We can be happy here."

"But Father won't approve."

She turned him to face her and looked him in the eye. "I am your wife and you are my husband, and I can't live with your father."

Mathew was struggling to find a reply.

"Mathew, you own twenty per cent of the company, your father signed the shares over when we married. What you are going to do is withdraw enough money to enable us to buy that lovely house."

She then kissed him.

They continued to discuss the plan all the way home. It took a while to break down his resistance. Over the course of the journey, Mathew's attempts to prevaricate became weaker with each point made. Mary's arguments that life would be much happier with a house of their own became stronger.

By the time they returned home and entered the bedroom she was aware his defences were holding on by a thread. She just needed to get him over the line. Mary led him across to the bed and pulled off his shirt. An hour and a half later as they lay in each other's arms Mathew said, "I'll speak to him tonight."

Mary had to dig her nails hard into the back of her hand to stop looking too jubilant.

*

That evening Mary stood out in the hallway; there were voices in the parlour. At first, Archibald's was raised, but to her great joy Mathew appeared to give as good as he got. The shouting match lasted for a full ten minutes but then it seemed to go quiet. Her heart was beating faster. The tension was killing her. A few minutes later she could bear it no longer. She entered the room. Her husband sat in an easy chair looking at his hands. Archibald crouched in front of the fire poking the coals.

"Ah Mary," said Archibald calmly. "I have just been explaining to Mathew that your idea for taking money out of the company to buy a house will never work."

He added another shovel of coal.

"Unfortunately, when I had the papers drawn up to give Mathew shares there is a clause saying you can only take out a maximum of £50 per year. You must invest all profit back in."

He gave the fire a prod.

"I'm sure if you check with our lawyer you will find that's the case."

Mary stood stunned, she was reeling and trying not to show it. Her heart sank. Mathew continued looking at his hands.

"Tell you what," said Archibald as he stood up with a smile. "How about I give you some money to redecorate your room. Spend a little time thinking what colour you would like. Get other ladies of the house involved. I'm sure you would all enjoy that, would be a nice project that would keep you busy for a while. Or the garden. There is a patch at the rear needing some attention. You can grow some plants while Mathew and I will get on with growing the family's wealth."

He went into his pocket, pulled out a small box and placed it on the table.

"And I know you have been a little upset so as a very special treat I've even bought you a lovely sapphire brooch."

He then picked up some papers and made to leave.

"Come, Mathew."

Mathew stood. Mary looked at her husband.

Mathew looked at the ceiling. He glanced at his wife then sheepishly looked at the floor, before following his father out of the room.

Historical Note

From the original harbour at the mouth of the river, Leith docks developed over a 137-year period as more land was reclaimed.

The old East Dock opened in 1806, the old West Dock in 1817. The Victoria Dock in 1852 allowed access for larger steamships. Then followed the Albert Dock in 1869, the Edinburgh Dock in 1881, the Imperial Dock in 1904 and the Western Harbour in 1943.

Chapter 18

The Raid

Junction St Bridge, Leith -2nd April 1916

"You look happy for once," said old Jock turning from the driver's seat, his craggy features curious. The rattle of milk bottles stopped. Daisy snorted and stamped.

"Aye" said Johnny from the back of the cart.

It surprised Johnny Preston to feel his face reddening. They had reached the halfway point of their round, the usual spot on the bridge on Great Junction Street. Keen to avoid any further conversation he leapt down to give Daisy her bag of oats.

Despite the early hour, there was already lots of activity downstream. Men pouring into Hawthorns engineering works and at Yoolls wharf on the right-hand bank of the river. On the opposite side at Innes shipyard, the coal yard and the railway were as busy.

A sunny morning, warm for the time of year. Even from their high vantage point, the slimy grey river stank from the effluent from the mills and other industry further up, that and much of Edinburgh's sewage.

Then came a clang from the drawbridge at Sandport, as it raised to let through a naval patrol boat. Vessels packed the port, the usual merchant craft on the river supplemented by almost as many from the Royal Navy. Cruisers and Minesweepers fought for space. In the distance Johnny saw the forest of masts from dozens of ships in the Victoria Docks further down. The war had brought a boom to the town, all the yards at full stretch repairing navy vessels of every shape and size. With so many men in France, there was work for all, women included.

As the bell from Saint Mary's struck seven Johnny gave old Jock a wave as he left the dairy stables. He ran to the tiny top-floor flat in Water Street, his long gangly legs bouncing up the rickety stairs. Today the usually languid Johnny appeared full of vigour. He burst into the shabby little kitchen ready for a quick breakfast before school, splashed a bit of water on his wide freckled face at the kitchen sink and passed his hand over his short fair hair, then sat with a thump on a stool at the narrow table.

His mother, in a threadbare apron and with the sagging face of a woman with too many troubles, stirred ladles into the boiling water on the range from a bag of oats. The sweet scent of hot porridge improved Johnny's mood even further. On the other side of the table sat Peter, his brother. Over a year older than Johnny at fifteen he looked very similar, just bigger in every way. He raised his eyes toward their mum as she continued to stir. *Here we go again* they said, as she turned to them and thumped a spoonful of gruel into their bowls.

"And as for you," she said, pointing her wooden spoon at Peter, "you're not too old to feel the back of my hand let me tell you."

"Give it a rest Mum," growled Peter looking into his bowl.

Johnny smiled to himself.

"Don't you tell me to give it a rest," she said, her voice rising. "After the effort my Frank made finding you an apprenticeship at the cooper's yard and you would simply throw it away."

At the table Peter was in the same foul mood he had been in for the past two days, still smarting after his recent humiliation. His mum had embarrassed him in front of all his friends by striding into the recruiting office and telling the sergeant his real age. Despite his protests she had grabbed him by the ear and dragged him home.

Johnny sat and ate his porridge in silence. He smiled again; he was happier than he could ever remember being.

"And look at your dad's twin, your poor Uncle Tony. He never even made it to the battlefield, killed in the train crash at Gretna only a year past with these other two hundred Leith lads." Her lips quivered. "Terrible, terrible. Do you want to end up like him?" She raised her wooden spoon and shook it at him again.

"It's difficult being a woman alone with you pair to bring up and your dad away in France." She tutted. "And the amount you eat… I love you boys but you're like a couple of pigs."

Christabel Thompson had spoken to Johnny yesterday. He still didn't quite believe it; he had been so taken aback he couldn't even remember what she had said. Today he had one goal in mind and that was to talk to her again. With his wages saved from his milk round he was going to ask her out tomorrow night to the film at the Gaiety in the Kirkgate.

"There's hardly anything in the shops with shortages getting worse all the time. At the butchers on Bernard Street the other day he wanted sixpence for some scabby looking sausages, a sixpence, would you believe it? I know there are lots of others in the same boat. Who knows where it's going to end."

Johnny stood and put on his jacket.

"Get you and give your face a proper wash before you go shooting off," snapped his mother. "And your neck. And remember your school books; you would forget your heid if it wasn't screwed on."

Johnny scrubbed his face with the bar of Sunlight soap at the grubby kitchen sink and brushed his teeth. He came back for his jacket, headed out the door and dashed down the stair. His mother noticed the pile of schoolbooks he'd left behind and shook her head in exasperation.

*

He made his way up Constitution Street, the major roads already busy with heavy lorries and horse-drawn traffic to-ing and fro-ing from the docks. The strong smell of alcohol filled his nostrils as he passed the whiskey bonds. The clatter of metal on metal from the ship repair yards, the factories, the works; it felt everyone was in a hurry, helping with the war effort.

Johnny hated school and couldn't wait to leave in the summer and get himself a trade like his older brother. He was useless at sums and spelling, and he spent most of his time there daydreaming. Today he had plenty to dream about.

Leith Academy had boys' and girls' sections, each with their own playground. Despite the wild commotion from games of skipping, football, hide and seek, hopscotch and marbles the two groups rarely got the chance to mix. Johnny spent many days looking at Christabel from a distance through the railings, and now he might be able to turn his dreams into reality. He had it all planned out. He had often followed her and her two friends home from school – she lived at the end of Baltic Street near the corner with Constitution Street opposite the entrance to the docks. Her friends always left her at Queen Charlotte Street and she made the last part of her journey on her own. He decided that would be when he would make his move.

Later that afternoon Johnny stared out of the high windows at the bright blue sky as the sun streamed into the drab classroom. Old "smelly" Brown was droning on about some diagram he'd put on the blackboard. This offered the perfect opportunity for Johnny to switch off. He started to think of the best way to approach his meeting with Christabel. In his mind he turned over the various scenarios of what he might say, how he might say it, what kind of expression he would have as he said it.

Johnny loved the cinema and pondered whether to style himself on either the dashing Douglas Fairbanks or more of a comedy approach based on Charlie Chaplin. As he swithered over this dilemma, he noticed a tapping sound. It seemed to get louder. Then he recognised the stale odour and when he turned old Brown loomed over him.

Mr Brown was a podgy little man in his mid-50s with ridiculously bushy eyebrows and a similar amount of hair coming out of his ears. On his head was a mortar board and under his gown his threadbare tweed suit, numerous old stains covering its front. He had sallow skin and a permanent scowl. To Johnny his scowl appeared even less welcoming than usual. His beady eyes drilled into him while he tapped the long leather taws with a steady rhythm against his calf.

"Ah Mr Preston, you have decided to join us," he said with a mock cheerfulness.

He paused; his voice hardened. "Where are your schoolbooks Preston?"

"Eh… I… Eh."

Brown's tone hardened further.

"What are you, Preston?"

"A fool sir," replied Johnny.

"A what?"

"A fool, sir."

"And why are you a fool, Preston?"

"Because I forgot my jotter, sir."

"And what happens to fools who forget their jotter."

"Belt, sir."

"How many?"

"Twelve of the best, sir."

Then Brown raised his voice to a shout. "So, what are you waiting for, come to the front!"

The boys at Leith Academy had to go through this humiliation on a near daily basis. All teachers used the belt, and it was obvious that a few, Mr Brown included, got some kind of perverse pleasure out of it. The boys could tell by the twisted smile on his lips as he delivered the punishment. The general view was that Mr Brown was quite mad. The rumour was that he'd had bad treatment when captured during the Boer War and the boys thought that he liked to take his revenge out on them.

Johnny stood up and walked in front of the blackboard, cringing as he anticipated what was to come. He held out his hand, and the class became silent apart from the whipping sound as Mr Brown warmed up with a few practice swings. He limbered up as if a champion boxer to get himself into the correct frame of mind to deliver the thrashing.

"Don't say I'm not kind to you, Preston," he said coldly. "As your father is away fighting the Bosh, you're only getting four on each hand."

He stared at Johnny with his familiar sneer.

"Well what do you say Preston?"

"Thank you, sir."

"But then you will stay behind after school for two hours detention," he said through his thin, twisted lips. Johnny's heart sank. Mr Brown took a short run up before bringing the belt down with a loud crack.

Mr Brown would later go to his damp, dingy flat in Dock Street and spend the evening on his own, drinking cheap whisky and reading the Greek classics, drink and concentration being the only effective way he had to keep away the demons.

After the beating Johnny rubbed his throbbing red hands, now hot and stinging. This was the worst possible scenario. The pain was nothing compared to knowing his plan to meet with Christabel was in tatters. After his detention that afternoon Johnny trudged home dejected. His plans had gone up in smoke. Today the school broke for holidays and he might not get another chance for weeks. What if she had forgotten him by then? That evening Johnny was morose as he sat moping in their spartan kitchen. He couldn't think what to do. He glanced out the window and noticed that the street lights were dimmed. Earlier there had been an air raid warning, no doubt another false alarm.

His mum arrived home and started bustling about. Johnny could tell she was in the mood where she could start moaning at him for the slightest thing. Knowing it was wise not to hang around, he slipped out the door. On the way downstairs he decided that the best thing to do was hang around the bottom of Constitution Street by the dock gates. Christabel might come out on an errand. There was little chance but he couldn't think what else to do. Darkness was falling but there was a half moon. Because of the air raid warning the police had switched off the traffic lights, and the streetlamps were lowered to give only the dimmest light. Johnny noticed that all the ships in the docks still had their lights on.

The church bell struck nine. He had been standing around the gates for two hours and it was getting cold. He was wasting his time and it would be as well to return home. It was now dark apart from the slight glow from the vessels in the harbour. He was about to head along Bernard Street when he became aware of a droning sound. It was unusual. It appeared to get louder. He peered up and down the street. He didn't recognise it. What might it be? He noticed two soldiers guarding the dock entrance were pointing up into the sky. He looked up and far above saw the outline of a what appeared to be a giant sausage crossing in front of the moon.

"What on earth is that?" he said aloud.

*

Six hundred and fifty feet above, Captain-lieutenant Alois Bocker was lost. His search for Rosyth dockyard had failed, and he had run out of options. It was time to take the L14 Zeppelin Airship home.

He spotted lights below and made a decision.

He shouted to his co-pilot to release the bombs.

*

Johnny's eardrums rattled as he staggered back. There was an ear bursting thud, then an enormous explosion a hundred yards along the road as flames licked up from the Timberbush. He reeled with shock. Seconds later he had to cover his head as broken tiles from the warehouse roofs came raining around him. He fell. Then another thump came from the direction of the Shore. There was a massive explosion and then huge sheets of flame spiralled high into the air from the Innes and Grieve Whiskey Bond.

Johnny picked himself up, stunned. People began to pour out of their houses into the street. Panic and screams, individuals running in all directions. The air raid siren began to wail. Johnny brought himself to his senses and started to run across Baltic Street toward home.

On the far side of the road people lurched in panic from Christabel's tenement stair. Then he saw her; she was alone and looked terrified as she stumbled out of the stair doorway. She glanced up and their eyes met. From the other side of the street Johnny ran towards her. Then another huge thud came from above. Johnny reeled from the blast. Looking up, he saw the roof of her tenement was crumbling and in flames. Masonry came thundering onto the pavement. A large piece of stone bounced up and hit him square on the chest sending him flying backwards. He lay on his back, winded and sore. Everywhere around him lay bricks, stones, and timber. Stone dust filled the air. His nostrils and mouth were thick with it .He heard more thuds and explosions, but they seemed to move away. He sat up, touched blood on his face and it was on his jacket. Slowly he got to his feet; he was dizzy. Cries and shouts came from all directions in the darkness, only the fires throwing any light. He stood up and looked around as the dust cleared.

On the other side of the road a shape was lying among the fallen masonry. He stumbled over the debris. In the rubble lay Christabel. Her lovely face was unmarked but her body lay broken and twisted into a grotesque, unnatural position. There was blood, lots of blood.

Johnny stood stock still and in shock, his face rigid. His jaw tightened. He knelt down beside her and caressed her hair.

"I wanted to see you, Christabel," he whispered.

Historical Note

On the evening of the 2nd April 1916 two Zeppelins reached the Firth of Forth while aiming to attack the Royal naval base at Rosyth. Lost in the darkness they made their way towards Edinburgh. The first few bombs landed in Leith; it was Scotland's first ever air raid. In total 24 bombs were dropped; 13 people were killed and 24 injured.

The Quintinshill (signal box near Gretna Green) rail disaster occurred on 22nd May 1915 and was Britain's worst ever rail disaster, killing 215 soldiers, most of whom were from the 1/7th (Leith) Battalion of Royal Scots en route to Gallipoli. They were buried in a mass grave in Rosebank Cemetery.

Chapter 19

The Aliens

Water Street, Leith -11th June 1940

"It was amazing Mum; came down with such a splash. Two Spitfires chased it; the Messerschmitt crashed right out in the middle of the Firth – Bang!"

"All right, all right; you have already told me enough of your afternoon's adventure. Now sit still and eat your tea."

The smell of fried spam brought a smile to Liz Preston's impish freckled face as her mum slapped the plate in front of her.

Liz, animated, her eyes never still, was full of stories of her day's adventure. For her mother it was her most endearing feature but sometimes she wished she could be a little quieter. Liz was a bouncing ball always bursting with energy. Her mum sighed, relieved at the brief silence as Liz stopped talking long enough to wipe her fingers on her white blouse and polish her fork on her green cotton skirt before shovelling the spam and powdered potatoes into her mouth.

A rumble came from the hallway, the door was thrown open and Liz's older brother lumbered into the small kitchen. Big-boned and brawny, he leaned over the table, grabbed the knife out of Liz's hand and lifted a heel of bread.

"Hey," said Liz and slapped at his arm.

He spooned jam on the bread and turned towards the entrance.

"Have to go."

"George, where are you going?" snapped her mum. "It's tea time."

"Got to get the tally bas..." the end of his last word lost as he stuffed the bread in his mouth. He stumbled out and headed down the stairs.

Liz watched him leave, her quick blue eyes narrowed.

"He is so annoying."

Her mother nodded, and then raised her tired eyes to the ceiling, exasperated.

"And I bet he's up to no good," said Liz.

Liz didn't like George; for as long as she could remember they'd rubbed each other up the wrong way. At fifteen, three years older and three times her size, he liked to throw his weight about but she stood up to him. She also knew (but ignored) that the constant friction between them caused her mother to despair.

This afternoon's escapade at the docks with Maria had been fun and she looked forward to seeing her again that evening. Liz and Maria loved the same things: peevers, scrapbooks, going on adventures, skipping and singing. They even appeared alike, tall and thin with the same style of long hair, though a difference in that Liz was fair and Maria dark. Often, they wore the same design of a print dress bought from the same draper's shop and sometimes were taken as sisters. The two had been inseparable since meeting on their first day at school.

They had talked of leaving next year and maybe getting a job together in the bottle factory like Liz's brother, although Maria thought her dad may say she would have to stay and work in their shop.

"I'm off to Maria's," called Liz.

"Be back before dark," said her dad, slumped in his armchair in an oil stained boiler suit, just home from another long shift at the shipyard. Liz saw it coming and slipped out the door before the fight started in earnest.

"Johnny Preston, look at the state of your boiler suit! Will you get your backside off my good chair!" screeched her mum.

The shouts receded as Liz scampered down the stairs. The year since the war began had passed in a flash. Liz had loved every minute. It wasn't frightening, just exciting. The main docks were a hive of activity. Today's dogfight over the Forth had been a bonus but the whole town was buzzing, a stream of ships, lorries, trains and soldiers and sailors coming in and out each day.

Liz waved as a convoy of tanks and field guns trundled along the Shore towards the docks. A clang came from the shipyards working flat out; her dad told her they launched a brand-new Corvette or Frigate every few weeks while others were constantly being repaired or refitted. Despite their arguments her mum was pleased that with her dad being a riveter at Robbs yard he had lots of extra overtime.

It had been a warm day with no wind but now a light sea mist blew in and she stopped to watch two swans and their seven little signets cruise majestically past the goods yard on the far side.

When she and Maria thought about it, the only bad thing with the war was the rubbish sweets available on your ration card. She headed towards Henderson Street and Maria's dad's ice cream shop. A smile crossed her lips at the notion of seeing Luigi, Maria's older brother. Maria had told her he was home on leave following the drama of his escape with thousands of others from Dunkirk only two weeks before. He had such a lovely laugh. Maria's house was warm and welcoming, unlike her own with its arguing and her big brother. She liked nothing better than helping Maria and her mum with baking while singing the street songs they knew.

The strong stink of diesel oil and grease filled the air from the Royal Navy Destroyer secured to the quayside; it showed the signs of heavy use, paint peeling and blistering in places. It had blast damage to its bridge. Sailors in their blue uniforms and little white hats had replaced the usual bustle of porters and stevedores loading and unloading. Pubs along the Shore were all bursting at the seams with servicemen

At the bridge at the foot of Henderson Street, she spotted George with three of his friends on the other side of the road. Something wasn't right; she knew him well enough to tell they were up to something. They had an aggressive bluster about them tonight, egging each other on. She recognised the body language. Liz crossed the road and seized her brother by the sleeve.

"What are you doing?" she said sharply.

George gave her a scornful look and shoved her away, full of bravado in front of his cronies.

"We are doing our patriotic duty so go you and play your hopscotch or with your dollies," he said with a sneer.

He turned to his friends. "Right boys, let's get the eyeties."

"Aye, tally bastards," said another.

"What are you talking about?" shouted Liz.

"Come on lads," said George ignoring her, "let's do them."

The group moved off and trotted up Henderson Street.

Liz shook her head in annoyance, her hackles rising. Why couldn't he have been the one evacuated instead of so many of her friends from school? Her class was now only half the size, with lots of them having been sent to the safety of the countryside. Neither Maria's nor Liz's mum would hear of such a thing.

From Henderson Street Liz turned into the Yardheads and was stunned by the sight before her. She took a sharp intake of breath at the shock. *What on earth were they doing?*

George and his friends were now with a much larger group of young men who had congregated across the road from Maria's dad's shop. They gathered together piles of rubble and bricks from a building site.

"Right lads let's see how they like British artillery," shouted George from the front.

Liz experienced a wave of disgust at the sight of him as the burly oaf swaggered around with menace. The realisation of what was going to happen hit her. A choked cry forced itself up from her throat.

Liz then looked on in horror as the first bricks arced through the air and plunged through the shop's main plate-glass window. Then came a cheer. Liz glanced up at the flat above and her heart broke as she saw Maria looking terrified as she watched the mob below. More missiles followed and hurtled through the window of the upstairs flat. More cheers with each direct hit. She heard Maria scream. Liz charged forward and grabbed her brother's arm.

"Stop it, stop it!" she screamed. "That belongs to Maria's family."

George pushed her away; she stumbled over rubble and fell onto her back.

"Dinny be daft Liz, they are only dirty eyeties," he snarled. "They deserve what's coming."

Liz shuddered as Maria's father and Luigi charged out of the shop's front entrance, her father shouting something in Italian with blood streaming down his face, armed with a brush pole; his son right behind him.

Liz stood up, helpless as George led the mob as it pushed forward. A violent scuffle broke out as punches and kicks flew. She watched on in horror as Maria's brother and father, badly outnumbered, were wrestled to the ground and took a beating.

Liz panicked; she was powerless. Then came the shrill blast of a whistle. She turned and felt a wave of relief as two uniformed police came briskly around the corner. She was glad to see the massive frame of the giant sergeant. *Thank God, nobody will mess with him.* The pack backed off, then there was a lull as Maria's brother and father clambered to their feet.

Then to Liz's amazement another cheer broke out as the sergeant handcuffed Maria's father and Luigi. Maria's mum came staggering out of the shop screaming. Maria was holding onto her apron, her eyes puffy with tears. The policemen batted her mother away and marched the two men off towards the Shore to the cheers of the youths.

Liz looked away. She turned and ran for home, her face hot with tears.

*

Later that evening Liz listened as George returned. His footsteps came towards the kitchen. She followed and crept in; he sat at the table making himself a sandwich. Sweaty and red faced with that smug look. Liz carefully lifted a large empty pot from the cooker and lifted it high. There was a loud clang as she smashed him over the head as hard as she could. He slumped to the floor stunned. Liz leapt on him scratching and punching.

"You … you monster," she screamed.

Her father came running in.

"What the hell is going on!"

Her father pulled her off and dragged her out of the room. The last thing she saw as the kitchen door swung closed was her brother laying squealing on the floor, blood pouring from his head.

*

Next morning there was a thin drizzle. Liz hesitated as she arrived at the shopfront. Smashed glass still littered the pavement. She knocked quietly and seconds later Maria's mother opened the door an inch. Liz was shocked to see she seemed to have aged ten years, her smiling face and bright shining eyes reduced to a dark and stunned grimace.

She let Liz in.

"She's upstairs," she said in her accented Scots and then turned away. This simple body movement told Liz that things were not as they had been. She sensed that they would never return to how they once were.

Liz followed her through the smashed shop then upstairs to the family's living room. Maria was curled up on the big red settee, the one upon which the two of them had spent many nights laughing and joking. Liz loved this room. Maria's mother was happy and funny, her dad smelled of spice and tobacco and gave her free sweets and even ice cream. She had always much preferred it to her own spartan house where her own mother often seemed too worn out to have time for her.

Liz sat next to Maria on the big settee. Her heart went out to her friend but she couldn't think of anything to do or say to make it better. Neither of them spoke.

When Liz looked back on this day (as she would most days in the future) she felt only confusion and shame. It made no sense to her whichever way she looked at it. Her best friend and her lovely family which Liz had almost been a part of had been beaten up, their property smashed, and her father imprisoned by her own neighbours, even by her own flesh and blood. It had to be a kind of madness. Things with her brother would never recover.

She peered around the room at the wreckage of the night before, then took Maria's hand and squeezed. The action seemed to bring Maria her out of her shocked state.

"Let's go down the Shore," said Liz.

They walked together hand in hand, Maria pale, her face chalk white. They said nothing until they reached Tolbooth Wynd and then, as if a dam had broken, the words just started pouring out of her.

"My mum's offie upset, they've taken my dad and brother to the jail. They claim we are aliens; I don't know what that means. We will stay with my auntie over in Glasgow; Mum says it's safer there.

Maria barely paused to take breath.

"And with ma brother in the army fighting for the British it doesn't make sense; I don't understand what's happening. What's this all about? I thought we were at war with the Germans but I'm now some sort of Italian and here was me thinking I was a Leither."

Liz squeezed her hand tighter.

"You are a Leither," cried Liz. "You're just like me, how can you not be. We were born here, we go to school here, we spend all our time here, our families live here, how can you not be?"

"They say we are Italians and that we like the Germans, but I've never even met a German. My big brother has been away attacking the Germans, has he been fighting the Italians as well? But how can he if we are Italians. I don't get it. What does it mean? Are Leithers fighting the Germans or are they fighting the Italians, but if we are both Leithers, how…"

Liz's tears of anger welled up.

"I don't care what they say," cried Liz, "you're ma best pal and you always will be. It's this stupid war, making everyone hate each other. You are a Leither and that's it – end of story."

They popped into old Maw Greens shop for one of her home-made lollipops. Maw Green was a grouchy old wifey but today she had changed; she even smiled when serving Maria. She looked embarrassed – she had heard what happened.

"When are you leaving?"

"Tonight."

"Will I not see you again?"

"No, not till this is over, but I want to come back."

"I hope you do," Liz stopped. "Fancy a game of peevers?"

"No." Then a thin smile appeared on Maria's lips. "But let's go skipping."

The rain had stopped, and the sun broke through as Liz and Maria held hands and skipped along the Shore towards the Docks.

Historical Note

During the conflict Robbs shipyard built forty-two vessels for the Royal Navy; frigates, corvettes and minesweepers. They also refitted and repaired nearly 3,000 ships belonging to the Royal Navy and Merchant Navy. They launched one new ship on average every six weeks and a vessel was repaired every day of this long and bloody conflict. Under great secrecy, parts of the Mulberry Harbour used at the D-day landings were also built in Leith.

The day after Mussolini had declared war on Britain Churchill gave the order "Collar the lot". This led to the internment of thousands of foreign nationals living in Britain, the vast majority of whom were innocent.

Chapter 20

The Fire

The Shore, Leith -4th November 1963

"To me Joe, to me," cried Billy as they manoeuvred the old chest of drawers out the door of the first-floor tenement flat. On the landing Joe's Aunt Maggie gyrated, mop in hand. The Beatles *She Loves You* played at full volume on her transistor radio as she vigorously cleaned.

Suddenly she stopped, concern on her face.

"Where did you get that bruise?" She gently fingered the tender swelling on Billy's face.

He looked away. "Eh … walked into a door."

She gave him a sympathetic glance. Pulled a threepenny bit from her pocket and squeezed it into his hand with a gentle smile. The boys dragged the chest to the bottom of the stairs and hauled it out onto the Shore.

"My uncle Tam always gets new furniture when he comes back flush from the whalers. Perfect timing for us," said Joe, his thin freckled face cheerful, full of enthusiasm.

Billy Preston was the taller of the two; fair, with a narrow face and large, sad blue eyes. Both boys had a short back and sides and dressed in khaki shorts and plastic sandals from Woolworths. They both wore the same grey school jumper.

The Shore was alive with noise. It appeared to come from every direction. Hammering from the cooperage and Browns yacht repair yard. A grinding from the coal chute at the docks or the high-pitched whine from the sawmill up the road. A throaty chug from a tug as it made its way towards the Firth.

The waft of spirit from the whiskey bonds seemed to clash with the smells of diesel oil and stale bilge water from the dilapidated coaster berthed at the quayside. The day was fine. A light west wind brought a hint of the scent of chocolate downriver from the Fry's factory at Powderhall. On the river, two swans glided majestically downstream. Further along the wharf, a group of seagulls squabbled over a dead rat.

They lifted the chest and dragged it passed Bill's Bar and the Ship Inn, on towards Slimons the Ironmonger.

"With the stuff we've got it's going to be the best ever," said Joe.

"Aye," replied Billy. "It will go down in the history books, the biggest ever in Leith."

"So long as we can hold on to it," said Joe with a concerned glance.

They dragged the chest around the corner into Burgess Street and up towards their base.

"Did you hear about McGraw?" said Joe.

"What?"

"He took on twelve of them and gave them a doing."

Billy gave a short, barking laugh. "Away and bile yer heid!"

"Am telling you it's true," said Joe, indignant.

"Were you there?"

"Aye," said Joe, then, after a moment's hesitation, "well naw, but I heard about it."

They stopped for a brief rest. Then a sudden cacophony of noises from the horns, sirens and whistles that announced lunchtime for the factories, bonds and yards all over the port.

"Look," said Billy, "I know Clinton McGraw is leader of the St Anthony's Lane mob and he is one of the hardest lads in Leith but twelve … come on."

"Am telling you," said Joe, "he's mental."

"Aye, you're right, but Big Hendo is on our side and he is even more mental – he would take McGraw no bother."

Who knows, maybe we'll soon find out," said Joe.

With one final effort they at last made it to the patch of waste ground in Water Street and threw the drawers onto the growing layers of old sofas, broken chairs and packing cases. They stood back and looked on, satisfied.

"It's huge," said Joe, "and that's only half of what we've got stashed away. I need to get home for dinner; I'll only be twenty minutes and I'll meet you back here."

Billy didn't fancy going home for dinner. His mum's latest would be there, a car mechanic from Porty, a great bear of a man. He rubbed his bruise and winced.

Billy's mum had had a whole string of them for as long as he could remember. But this one was the worst yet. There was that tailor from Junction Street. He wasn't exactly friendly but at least he had given him that nice jacket.

Then that slimy little weasel from the fish processor, who stunk the whole house out with that smell. Then that electrician who worked at Robbs shipyard. His mum had chucked him out when Billy's big sister Veronica had said she would leave (which she did soon afterwards anyway and moved in with his dad, George). But this new one was by far the worst; a real nasty piece of work.

Joe and Billy were best of pals in primary four. There was a third member of their group, wee Alec. Miss McCafferty their old wifey teacher even referred to them as "The Three Musketeers", they appeared so inseparable. Yet in the latter half of October they became sworn enemies. With wee Alec living a few streets away in Henderson Street he was part of the St Anthony's mob, and when it came to bonfire night, normal rules did not apply.

Along with the other kids living around the Shore and Water Street the boys had been busy for weeks. The fire was their finest yet in the battle to have the biggest in Leith. They had scavenged everywhere, around the cooper's yard, on the docks, around Yorkies scrapyard; they had even combed the beach more than once. The boys and their comrades had travelled far and wide in their quest.

To an onlooker they appeared a rabble of kids, but were actually highly organised. Leaders, lookouts, and scavengers all worked together with the single aim of collecting as much flammable material as possible. The excitement had been building for days, yet today there was also a real tension in the air. It was a dangerous time; they were now at their most vulnerable to attack.

After Joe had gone Billy nipped to the bakers and spent his threepence on a scotch pie. He sat on an old battered settee along with the three younger boys on guard duty.

Joe soon returned with a few of the others when Billy spotted older boys coming out of Queen Charlotte Street.

"Look out, its Hendo," he said quietly.

The atmosphere changed. Big Arthur Henderson walked with a swagger onto the waste ground. At fifteen he already had the beginnings of a beard. He carried a cudgel made from an old bannister with a nail sticking out of one end, making a lethal weapon.

Tall, his big ears accentuated by his swept back duck's-arse hairstyle. He had a long scar on his forehead, full lips and a wide, thuggish face. He wore a denim jacket. The words love and hate were tattooed amateurishly across his knuckles. He was accompanied by his two sidekicks, both with that scrawny, feral look, a sinister stare in their dark eyes.

Hendo was the "hard man" and undisputed leader of the pack. The boys knew big Arthur's reputation – they had listened to the stories of his fearsome fighting abilities. Billy felt dread creeping through his body as Hendo seemed to single him out and looked him up and down with a steely stare.

"All right wee man," he said, his smile not meeting his eyes.

Billy stood and the others took a step back.

"Take some lads and get up the Kirkgate, find what else you can," said Hendo.

Billy sprang into action. Along with Joe and a couple of younger kids he set off up Giles Street, glad to be out of the unpredictable Hendo's presence.

At the bottom of the Kirkgate they scrambled under the hoardings surrounding the demolition site.

The Kirkgate was barely recognisable from the bustling street Billy remembered from only a few months before; it now looked like a bomb had hit – a ghost town, derelict and gloomy. Broken masonry littered the street along with rusted bits of metal and broken glass. Wooden beams stood like the ribs of old wrecked ships. The buildings were in ruin but some shopfronts were still standing. *Poulsen and Smart, Drapers,* read one, *Kinnard's Tearooms*, *Claud Alexander, Tailors.* Further up, the sagging stalls of the Gaiety Theatre were still visible through a gap in the wall. Half the sign for Rocio's Café next door hung like a dying skeleton. But the pickings were rich; there were old bits of wood everywhere. They loaded up with as much as they could carry and soon returned to base with their arms full.

Hendo was still there when they got back, as other scavenging groups straggled back into the waste ground with plunder from elsewhere.

"I've got another job for you, wee man," said Hendo. "We know the St Anthony's team are on the prowl, so I need you to be on lookout, any problems, put out the call. Only one day to go; it's a dangerous time."

The thin light started to fade and as it was now tea time most of the kids began to wander home. They left Billy on guard and alone. All was quiet. It was cold. He stamped his feet and rubbed his hands to stop himself shivering. He was thinking of where he might get something to eat when he saw them.

At first it was only one. Billy recognised him immediately from school. Despite the dim light his body language made it obvious he was scouting, the way he crept along the wall. Then there was another. The third was wee Alec, but the fourth was one of their big lads. This was it, the St Anthony's mob; this was a raid, and it looked a big one at that.

Billy turned and grabbed the two old pots he had in place and ran off down Water Street screaming and clattering them together as loud as he could. Hendo had planned well. Within a few seconds kids came teeming out of the stairs. Cudgels prepared in advance were brought forward. Strategically placed piles of stones and rocks were distributed.

The invaders poured around the corner from Tolbooth Wynd. Within less than a minute there were fifty or sixty kids at each end of the street. They eyed each other; the battle lines drawn. Although the St Anthony's squad had the greater numbers Hendo had chosen his ground well. The narrowness of the wynd meant that the St Anthony's crew struggled to bring all their numbers to bear.

Tension rose as the standoff continued. Then the St Anthony's hard man Clinton McGraw appeared at the front of his group. He was big and lumbering compared to the lithe Hendo. With a cry McGraw charged towards the Water Street boys as Hendo took up a defensive stance to meet him.

"This is huge," cried Billy.

"It's just like Bannockburn," shouted Joe.

A brick came flying over from the St Anthony's side and hit the boy who stayed at number nine. A scream and real blood. Then all hell let loose. Stones, bits of wood, bangers and even a rocket cascaded off a tenement wall. The melee soon became a running battle up and down the street. At one point Billy saw Hendo and Clinton McGraw go head to head but then they were soon lost in the maelstrom. A few adults came rushing out of their stairs, angry and shouting. Within seconds the battle lines started to melt away.

Then Billy saw him on the other side of the street, the big mechanic; how could you miss him? As both sides started to fall back Billy picked up a half brick. He judged the distance and then threw it with all the strength he could muster. In apparent slow motion the brick arced over the heads of those still going at it hand to hand. A jolt of adrenaline coursed through Billy as the mechanic looked up at the crucial moment and the half brick landed square on his nose. He staggered back, howling in pain. Billy could see blood spurting through his upheld fingers.

A wave of pure joy coursed through him as he fell back with the others to the safety of their patch. What a result. A direct hit.

There was an exhilaration among the Water Street kids now. Fired with adrenaline as they animatedly compared stories of the battle, jubilation that they had fought off the danger, their fire would be safe. Among several walking wounded, two boys with head injuries even had to go to hospital. The battle would be etched on the memory of participants for years to come although it lasted but a minute. Many years later old men reminisced over dominos and pints of beer about the battle of Tolbooth Wynd.

That night when Billy got to the door of his mum's shabby flat in Water Street, he took off his shoes and tiptoed past his mother's bedroom. He crept into the kitchen, made a sandwich and poured a glass of milk. He slipped into his room and lay on the bed; he could hear the mechanic through the wall in his mother's room next door. A gentle, regular groan.

Billy smiled, put his hands behind his head, and thought glorious thoughts.

Historical Note

Around 85 bonded warehouses stood in Leith in the 1960s. These matured around 90% of all Scotch whisky. The last bond, on Water Street, closed around 1995.

The Last whaler voyage from Leith was in 1963. It brought to an end an industry going back almost 350 years to 1616.

In the days before health and safety regulations the children of each neighbourhood would build their own bonfire.

Chapter 21

The Go Gos

Leith Academy -22nd May 1974

Billy Preston crept along the geography corridor. He thought about last night.

"I love you," she had said as she laid her hand on his chest.

At that moment it sunk in. He had a real dilemma on his hands. Big Stu was waiting at their usual spot around the corner from the chemistry labs.

"It's a load of shite mind you," whispered big Stu.

"What is?"

"Half a ton." He gave a silent laugh.

Billy raised his eyes at the bad joke then put a finger to his lips as they continued gingerly down the passage. It had come as a surprise when he bagged off with her a few weeks before at the final year disco. God, she was nice. He still found it hard to believe he'd cracked it with Georgina McKay. Billy needed to decide. *Was it going to be Georgina? And her hair, her mouth, her smell, and that moaning sound she made during their last snog. Or not? Or could he have both?*

"Soon be the next bell," said Stu, "then we can go for it."

Friday at 11 a.m. after the third period, the ideal time to head for the docks and the lunchtime action. All they needed was give the deputy headmaster (well known to be a total bastard and not daft) the slip as he patrolled the corridors that offered the best escape routes.

There was doubt in Billy's mind.

"Phone me at six and you will be round by seven," she had said. Not come around at seven, or would you please pop round at seven but "you will be round".

He could tell her dad was not happy, but he had managed a snog on each of the three times he'd been to her place. She let him push his hand up her jumper twice but it was now clear he wouldn't get any further without some kind of commitment. Being Friday, he may have to choose before the night was over. *Was it worth it?* It might take an awful long time and effort to get into her pants.

They stooped under the glass window on the door of maths room 5 and into the foreign languages' corridor, then all they had to do was head along the passage straight to the fire exit and freedom.

Like a scene from a horror movie, a loud voice boomed along the passage.

"Mr Preston and Mr Archdeacon."

The boys stopped in their tracks and turned. Major Bruce appeared like a spectre as if by magic from behind a cleaner's cupboard. He stood with the same straight back as on a parade ground in India thirty-five years earlier. His large shiny head didn't fit well with his huge handlebar moustache. Steely dark eyes bored into them. His black gown billowed behind him as he strode forwards. Though hidden the boys knew that positioned on his shoulder under the gown was his thick leather taws, an implement made in a factory in Lochgelly in Fife. With its twin prongs it was an object designed to inflict maximum pain.

"And where do you think you two are you going?" he said as he eyed them like a cat that had cornered a mouse.

"Eh ... eh ... taking a message to Mrs Clark," stammered Stu.

The Major's eyes narrowed.

"My arse," he said with the tightest of smiles. "Return to your class. I know you may leave us soon but it's not too late to give you both six on each hand." Then with a simple movement he let his gown ruffle to expose the taws. They knew the routine.

"Yes sir," they said in unison, turning back up the passageway as fast as possible.

Once out of sight they nipped into the graffiti covered boys' toilets. It stunk, but they waited. They'd learned from experience it was only a matter of time; all they needed to do was stall until the Major made his first catch. It only took a few minutes before they overheard him marching up the passage with a couple of third years (no doubt using his usual technique of a firm grip on their ear), his Sergeant Major parade ground voice ranting to the miscreants a likelihood of belting, expulsion and god knows what else.

"Old Radge," whispered Stu as they heard him pass. They retraced their steps and popped out the fire escape, a quick dash dipping low under the school kitchen windows and freedom. They lit up their number sixes as soon as they made their escape and headed towards the Shore.

"Ya beauty, Friday afternoon and doon the docks for the Go Go's," said Billy as they jogged down Constitution Street

"Aye, brilliant, we should be there for Stevie and Davie getting out."

There was the strong odour of spirits as they passed the whiskey bonds and warehouses that lined Water Street. Some still bustled with activity but others stood empty and neglected, waiting for investment that didn't appear to be coming anytime soon. With the three-day week only recently ended and high unemployment the prospects in the town were very limited. Only ten years earlier Leith had been a thriving port. Billy remembered as a child walking this same path with his mum. The smells of timber and the clang of hammers on steel. Now the place was quieter, it had a dilapidated feel. Shabby disused sheds and factories, broken windows and pipes, large areas of damp on walls and rotting wood.

Their two pals Davie and Stevie left school the year before and became apprentices at Robbs the shipbuilder, the only yard operating in Leith. As far as Billy could tell it sounded as if the lads spent most of their day trying to avoid work as much as possible while there were gory stories of industrial accidents, of drinking and far too many hard men for Billy's liking.

Billy much preferred the idea of a college or university – he only required three more Highers to be accepted. He knew he was lucky that his old man didn't earn enough so he would get a full student grant. Needed to reinvent himself. Much though he loved his pals it was time to move on. Leith was on the way down; time for somewhere new.

Studying politics was his plan, the lure of the far left. The Labour party couldn't resolve the problems of a place like Leith. It was the fat cats sitting up in Edinburgh in their bungalows who were the problem, them and the posh English (and Edinburgh) public-school toffs and worst of all the Yanks.

But he now had the added complication of Georgina to consider. He remembered he needed to call her by six. His dad, a Labour voter all his life just didn't get it, he even thought the Yanks should be in Vietnam.

"It's like dominoes, one goes and they all go," would spout old George, gone to seed, his fat frame sat in his chair in his cardigan with a can of beer and chain-smoking roll ups. Such an idiot – though Billy had to admit it was better than living at his mums. "And it's about time you had another haircut," he'd drone.

They needed more strikes; the miners had shown what might happen if the workers took over the means of production. He had tried to explain this to the guys during their dope-filled evenings but they were all just too daft to understand it.

"You see it's all about world domination by the capitalists, and their oppression of the masses," he'd explain. Billy knew this to be true as he had read it in the Morning Star newspaper belonging to his older brother who was a paid-up member of the socialist worker party.

Much to his annoyance the most common retort from the boys was, "Stuff your politics up your arse, and stop bogarting that joint ya tit."

Much as he loved them, they didn't get it, a couple of them already well on the way to being alcoholics like their fathers. With a drinking culture in the yards and factories it was hard not to develop a habit. Despite their lack of political awareness, he enjoyed hanging out with them most nights round Stevie's flat in Water Street. That was the centre of their social life, while a common love of hash, LSD, and Led Zeppelin kept their relationship strong.

Friday afternoons were special for the lads. Leith was all old shabby buildings. Industrial decay on a grand scale, crap beer, old man pubs, street walkers, gangs of football heavies and new ugly concrete blocks of flats that replaced the once atmospheric Kirkgate. It had become a miserable, dingy and depressing place but for 18-year-old boys it still offered a range of very interesting attractions.

Billy was unaware that come the future the streets around the Shore would be introduced to the joys of pasta, salad dressing, German lager and avocado sandwiches. Those days were a way off; but what it did offer was cheap beer, whisky and dark rum and the chance to see half-naked women.

On Friday afternoons when Robbs yard turned out for the weekend the pubs came alive as industrial workers from the factories and yards spilled out attracted by drink and Go-Go dancers. Despite their shabbiness, many bars flourished and a few fancier ones had proper stages or even cages which offered the dancers some protection.

But these were not for them; their favoured bar with its cheaper beer was in Carpet Lane. They arrived at the door at the same moment as Stevie and Davie

"All right bawbag," said Stevie, with a welcoming smile.

"Ok knob-end," replied Billy. They reserved this term of endearment for Stevie who with his handsome dark looks was the only one who (until Billy's luck with Georgina) had any success with girls.

Similar welcomes bounced between them as they entered the crowded bar, already full of shipyard workers and sailors. The stink of sweat, diesel oil and cigarette smoke filled the room, the pub far from salubrious. Black walls, sticky carpet and stinking bogs. The at one time beautiful white corniced celling was now a deep brown, stained with tobacco from thousands upon thousands of cigarettes.

Most of the clientele including Dave and Steve dressed in overalls and boiler suits but not Billy and Stu. They were "freaks" and proud of it. They looked with disdain on the "straights" with their short hair and did their best to avoid "heavies". Billy wore the uniform of ex-army combat jacket and bellbottomed loon pants. He was particularly keen on his new white platform shoes – one joy of being in their final year was that they didn't have to wear school uniform, one irritation being the still daily battles with his old man over the length of his hair.

Life was all about getting drunk and stoned, finding new cooler bands and all they now lacked were a few loose women. Billy's concern being that it appeared Georgina wouldn't be loose enough.

The entertainment was yet to start. At the bar they ordered four pints of McEwan's from the grizzled bar woman, fag hanging out of her mouth, it being well known she kept a baseball bat behind the bar to encourage any troublemakers to leave.

A drunk, emaciated woman in her forties tapped Billy on the shoulder. "Are you dancing son?" she pushed her wizened frame up against him.

Billy didn't know where to look.

"B … b … but there's no music."

Before anyone could answer a fight started at the next table between two rough looking hookers over the drunk Norwegian sailor sitting between them. A cheer went up among the patrons at the unexpected entertainment and it was a relief for Billy when the bar staff wrestled them out along with the woman who'd accosted him.

The entertainment began. A Go-Go dancer stepped onto the makeshift stage to ragged cheers from the crowd as Gary Glitter's *do you want to be in my gang* came through the tinny speakers.

"Fucks sake, it's Anne McGregor," said Davie looking shocked.

"Christ aye, she used to be two years above me," said Stu.

"I don't believe it," said Billy, his eyes widening.

“She stays down the stair from me, she’s pals with my big sister Veronica. Hey Stevie, did you not get a bag off with her that night doon at the school disco?”

Stevie gave a disdainful look, “Naw it wis her wee sister, ah nearly got ma hole in the changing rooms but then that bastard Major Bruce chased us out at the crucial moment.”

Anne wore a cheap purple nylon bikini with glitter she had added herself. She had short legs, small breasts and a podgy stomach. Her eyes were a bit too close together and covered in heavy, badly applied makeup, her brown hair stood rigid with hairspray. She started gyrating with an enthusiastic but poor imitation of a Pan’s People dance from Top of the Pops the week before. The throng gave a thin cheer.

The second dance was a slow number, Elvis. Halfway through the song a particularly sleazy looking guy in his forties stretched forward and stuck his hand under her bra and had a rough grope; he drew her onto his lap. Anne screamed, pulled herself away and fled the stage to coarse laughs and jeers from the crowd.

“Brilliant,” said Stu.

“No very classy,” said Davie.

“Mingin’,” said Billy.

He looked at the clock. He needed to phone Georgina in a few hours.

Three pints later and they moved on. Stevie had produced around fifty metal discs that he had made on his lathe at work. These were exactly the same size as credit tokens designed for the fruit machines found in pubs. The boys worked their way through the bars along the Shore and up Bernard Street and then Constitution Street. By crowding round each machine, they could feed in the counterfeit tokens and despite the low return could quickly clear out all the cash. Soon they had enough to keep them in booze and drugs for the whole weekend. The beer in most pubs was Tartan Special, McEwan's or Tennent's lager; given the long brewing tradition the poor quality was another sign of decay. Although a glimmer of hope had arrived in the shape of eighty shillings.

"I was reading about these guys who said there was great beer in the olden days," said Stu. "Pubs even used to make their own and they're trying to bring it back."

"That'll never happen," said Billy.

"Big business is making a fortune selling us this crap, I'm telling you, it's the Yanks, these dudes who run the council and the cops are all in their pocket. They're all in the masons. It's the rich guys that cause the problems."

The others raised their eyes and shook their heads.

At the last pub Billy watched the clock as it made its way round to six o'clock. It was decision time.

"Are you coming to score?" said Stevie.

Billy thought, *Was he? Or was he going to phone Georgina and go to hers?*

*

Later that night the LSD kicked in as they sat on the quayside outside the seamen's mission at the far end of the Shore. The last rays of the sun hit the harbour wall on the other side and glinted on the rough stone. There was a smell of salt, seaweed and sewage. Two swans glided upriver.

"Leith light," said Stevie. "Far out."

"It's beautiful, man," said Billy.

"Man," said Davie, "Leith is a shithole man, always been a shithole and always will be a shithole."

"Heavy, man," said Big Stu.

"But I still love it," said Stevie.

"Wow, man," said Billy pointing at the bare stone on the other side of the slow-moving river. "Look at that."

Historical Note

Robbs shipyard closed in 1983, the last in a history of shipbuilding in the town going back 600 years.

Chapter 22

The Little Pearl

The Shore, Leith -3rd May 2018

Although she had walked the same path many times before, Veronica Preston couldn't remember ever getting so much pleasure from the journey as she did today. That morning at breakfast she realised that this might be the first time she would have the upper hand in over forty years; yes, last time it must have been not long after they left school.

It was sunny, only a light breeze from the west and warm for the season. Almost a holiday atmosphere by the river. The cafes and bars along the Shore full of people sitting outside eating their avocado sandwiches with their lattes and sipping from their glasses of unpronounceable Belgian lager.

She stopped on the bridge on Bernard Street and looked down as the water meandered towards the Firth. How Leith had changed within her own lifetime, the floating restaurants on one side creating such a different atmosphere from the working ships and bustle she remembered in her youth. The smells and sounds now changed too. Much quieter, no longer any clanging of metal upon metal from the shipyards and factories and no more overpowering smell of maturing whisky from the bonds by her Water Street flat or diesel oil and grease from the vessels. On the north side a pair of swans and their eight cygnets cruised in a neat formation, occasionally dipping their heads in the water, so cute.

Veronica realised that she could already sense a slight tension, but it wasn't unpleasant. She continued along Sandport and on to Victoria Quay before entering the usual coffee spot for their regular monthly meet up.

She was relieved to discover that, although she was a little late, Anne had not yet arrived, so she ordered the customary plate of cakes and a cappuccino and moved over to the comfy leather armchairs by the window. Minutes later Anne stumbled in, full of apologies.

"The traffic is terrible," she blurted as she made her way across the room and lowered her ample proportions into the seat on the other side of the table. "Even the car park by the Scottish office building is packed. I wish they had bigger parking spaces for those of us with larger cars, it's such a tight fit if you have one like mine."

Veronica looked up with a wintery smile, but noticed that for a millisecond Anne glanced down and Veronica was at once painfully aware that again she herself wore that shapeless old Crimplene dress purchased from Primark some years previously.

In contrast, Anne looked resplendent in an obviously brand new, beautiful tailored lime green trouser suit with gold buttons, almost certainly from Boden. Veronica made a mental note not to mention it – which she knew would annoy Anne intensely. She as usual also wore that stunning sapphire ring—it sparkled in the light coming through the window—but no surprise that she'd got the shoes horribly wrong; pink slingbacks with open toes. Like ten fat little sausages, some even with a faint shadow of dark hair. Yuck.

When they were young Veronica had been the nice looking one, the one who got most of the male attention—too much as it turned out—while Anne always had that gormless look. Veronica thought it was because her eyes were a bit too close together and thinking back Veronica remembered she also had terrible skin then. This had probably only now improved due to the huge amounts she spent on regular treatments. It was hard to believe her younger brother Billy once told her he saw her working as a dancer at a bar in Carpet Lane back in the day. As youngsters Anne had not been popular at school and they only became acquainted because they both lived in the same stair in Water Street and their mums were good friends. But then life came along.

The two old school friends soon slipped into the normal routine, Anne animated as always. Her chair protested as it creaked under her—there was no other way of saying it— fat frame as she lurched for the nicest looking of the tray of cakes. Veronica by contrast was slim and neat. On her thin, wrinkled face, the remnants of what had once been a great beauty.

After the initial pleasantries about the weather they moved onto the familiar array of subjects and opinions (more often than not Anne's opinions, Veronica noted). They started as always with soft furnishings. Anne only yesterday had bought a couple of new cushions (in a sort of magenta tweed) and was giving serious consideration to a whole set of quality curtains for the dining room. She was having a real dilemma over both the fabric and the colour and she'd visited several high-class shops at Ocean Terminal as well as up in Edinburgh. She found the staff particularly surly and unhelpful at one of the Ocean Terminal stores.

"Don't know where they find them; wouldn't have got away with it in my day."

Veronica knew she was by far the more intelligent. After they quit school, she started building what she expected to develop into a successful career in financial services. Anne meanwhile married young, to that skinny little runt of a man with the big nose who lived at Maritime Lane. But, sod's law, it turned out that the skinny little runt of a man surprised everyone by becoming one of the most successful entrepreneurs in town and rumour had it was now a millionaire who owned a nationwide plumbing supplies business.

Then it was onto Leith's expensive fancy restaurants that Anne had visited over the past few weeks.

"Well, the rolled herring in Martin Wishart's had a vastly superior sauce to the one in Fishers, really quite a significant difference, think it came down to the amount of garlic, or maybe the touch of paprika. However, with the sweets it's the opposite. Fishers' profiteroles win every time. A much lighter pastry. It's all very so difficult," she said with a frown. "Given the prices they charge you really should expect perfection every time. Anyway, we are going to try the new Italian tonight."

Veronica's thoughts briefly turned to the "savers" curry in her fridge for this evening's meal. Not that she was bitter.

Anne then moved onto her views on Jeremy Corbyn and the future of the Labour party (not good) and then to a function she'd attended at the Malmaison Hotel with her husband. While there she learned of the shocking behaviour of the children across the road from one of her other friends (who actually lived in Haddington).

It was fair to say that the last forty years had not gone so well on the personal front as far as Veronica was concerned. She had to acknowledge that she had gone on to have three spectacularly unsuccessful marriages to very handsome but totally useless men who over time robbed her of her money, her career, and eventually her looks.

Veronica managed to get a word in and briefly turned the conversation to her own family, her grandchildren and her brother Billy's boy Gabriel, who was now doing well at college. Then the next-door neighbour's cat and how annoying it was when it messed on the potted plants outside her tenement door. She'd tried everything, pepper, a proprietary brand stuff; nothing seemed to work

As Veronica's brief interjection came to an end, she noticed that her palms were sweating a little more than usual, and that her mouth was a bit dry. *Was she ill?* Slowly the realisation dawned that this was in fact a sensation of anticipation and the beginnings of a rising excitement.

By now Anne had shifted onto her regular tirade about the Archers on BBC Radio 4. "Shocking, it's all going downhill."

Then to the declining quality of many fabrics for clothing even in more expensive shops, in particular for the more mature woman. Despite this blatant attempt to draw attention to her new clothes Veronica made a specific point of not mentioning the new trouser suit.

Veronica slowly become aware that for once she was actually enjoying this meeting; she sensed a tension building in her abdomen.

Anne was now in full flow. First, she complained her new hairdresser, who was Romanian and bisexual, had put up his prices. Followed by a long rant about the ridiculous parking charges in the town centre and then commenting on the design of the flats that replaced the last of the swathes of derelict warehouses that had come down in Leith over the past few years. Then moaning that she couldn't always get parked because of the numbers of tourists visiting the Royal Yacht Britannia.

Veronica experienced a heightened awareness. She was now acutely conscious that at any time of her choosing, she might do it – she would be able to drop in her little pearl.

Anne started her usual moan about immigration which Veronica had heard lots of times before of course – she could have repeated it word for word if necessary.

"How can you fit into the British way of life if you have a bag over your head?" Anne spluttered, sending a spray of crumbs from her third scone over the table.

"What we need is Boris in charge, then we will show them."

Yes, Veronica thought, that little pearl of gossip. That little pearl of gossip that would bring Anne's world crashing down. That little pearl of scandal that would enable Veronica to grind Anne's smug, fat face—along with her fancy German car, and her holidays in the Seychelles, and her stupid ugly smelly little lap dog—into the dust with her heel.

The only question now was when. She was aware of her heart beating faster and the sweat on her brow. Veronica had opportunities, the most obvious being when Anne took a brief break to stuff the last of the French fancies between her fat, flabby lips. Veronica felt her heart pounding with excitement as she came within a millisecond of letting it out.

Then she paused. She drew a deep breath; she couldn't do it. This feeling was far too good, this was a euphoria she had not experienced before and she knew for certain she wanted to experience it again.

I'll leave it until next month, thought Veronica.

Historical Note

The decision to build Victoria Quay, the large Scottish government building, in 1995 was the starting point in the regeneration of Leith. Many other developments have followed including Ocean Terminal while the arrival of the Royal Yacht Britannia added further to the attractions of the port. More will likely follow with the extension of the trams.

Chapter 23

The Family

Water Street, Leith -23rd February 2099

"**H**e what?"

"He wants to make his own decision," said Callum's father with an expression of incredulity.

The room quietened; Callum blushed. Big Uncle Nicholas threw back his head and let out a loud bellowing laugh. Others followed and soon the whole table was in hysterics.

Today was a special occasion to celebrate Callum's old great grandad Gabriel's 100th birthday. It was also a rare gathering of the entire Preston clan. As well as his mum and dad, there was his Uncle Peter and Aunt Mary, Big Aunt Jean and wee Uncle Thomas. Auntie Isobel and fat Uncle Nicholas. Uncle Joseph and skinny Aunt Maggie, little Uncle Alexander and tubby Aunt Esmerelda. All Callum's cousins were there: wee Rab, Adam, big Ralph. And the girls, Catherine, Marion and Margery who all sported the latest fashion of multiple large sapphire clasps woven into their hair (all created in the kitchen micro cloner, and copied from the jewel Callum's mum came across a few weeks before in the monthly market on the Shore). The family crammed around the table of Grandad's flat on the top floor of the nondescript new twenty-eight-storey block in Water Street.

"Why on earth would you want to do that?" said Uncle Nicholas, looking serious, his chair creaking as it struggled to accommodate his fat frame.

"Is that not illegal anyway?" chipped in Uncle Joseph, his flabby features quivering.

"And the act of a moron," said cousin Adam in his usual smartarse way with his lopsided smile, and his hair in the latest men's style, a "tonsure" with a close shave in the middle of his scalp.

"I don't care," replied Callum, looking flustered and pulling his hand through his shaggy hair. "That's what I want to do, so that's what I'm going to do."

Uncle Nicholas shook his head and looked around the table, using it as an excuse for a good sideways glance at Aunt Maggie for whom he'd always secretly had a bit of a thing.

"But seriously, I don't understand, how did this situation come about anyway?" said wee Uncle Thomas, scratching his large bald dome, nonplussed.

"You wouldn't believe it," said Callum's mum as she gave her son a withering stare.

Uncle Nicholas smiled at her. He still struggled to fathom how a wee bochle like Callum's dad could have captured so stunning looking a woman. Voluptuous despite her age, with long dark hair, and beautiful round hazel eyes. As always, she dressed with style, this time in the latest stunning bright red Prussian designer dress (that during the first course had been a shade of light blue).

"Might end up with a crazy murderer in the family; the whole idea is absolutely ridiculous."

"Look," said Callum louder than he intended, "it's simple." His face reddened. "I was down at the Shore walking along the top of the new flood defence walls. You know, next to that automatic boom that they put in after Portobello went under."

Uncle Nicholas nodded.

"Being January, it was roasting, so I bought an ice cream and down comes this Uberskyauto. The door slides open and out she walks." A dreamy expression crossed his face as he remembered the moment. "That was it – love at first sight; no argument."

Cousin Catherine giggled, Aunt Isobel looked exasperated, Uncle Thomas grimaced, and Uncle Peter looked confused.

"Young folk today, I don't know," said Callum's dad stabbing a piece of broccauliflower in frustration. Uncle Nicholas looked at his brother-in-law and they both shrugged.

"Listen son," piped up little Uncle Alexander from the other end of the table

Uncle Alexander was the brains in the family. As small as Callum's dad with frizzy hair and a goatee beard, he wore the latest scanner spectacles. He was the only one not on guaranteed wage allowance and had a proper job at the databank. The others tended to listen to him.

"I know you need to be your own man and all, but take a step back, examine the logic." His brows creased. "If your mother decided to get a new kitchen, does she go and physically visit lots of different kitchens and then choose one?" He eyed Callum with a quizzical glance. "No, she doesn't. What she does is tell the device exactly the type she wants. Then she trusts the Amazongram to deliver the best choice. Your mum would be aware that it's better than anything she could even imagine thinking up on her own."

He looked to Callum's mum and smiled, as did she – he, along with Uncle Thomas, Uncle Peter, Uncle Joseph and Aunt Isobel secretly had a thing for her. Meanwhile, unknown to him Aunt Maggie had always had a thing for him, Aunt Jean a thing for Uncle Joseph, Uncle Thomas a thing for Aunt Mary and Aunt Esmerelda a thing for both Callum's dad and cousin Catherine.

He looked serious again. "If you plan to watch a movie do you go and wade through the millions of films ever made to find what you fancy? No, you don't, you describe to the device what you wish to see and you trust the FlixNet to select the best option." Uncle Alexander pointed at the wall and the screen appeared "There. It's the same with everything else. This food we are eating, could we have such a spread without the BigEatagram? He pointed again. "And this?" he lifted the glass of Ginvod in front of him. "Boozlebook."

He cast his eyes around the room.

"If you want wallpaper you ask the Wallpaperapp, if you want a carpet it's Carpetgram, if you wish to bet on a race its LadbrokeHillapp and so it goes on."

He gave Callum a derisive stare.

"The fact of the matter is that the device is never wrong, whether you use the one under your fingernail, the one in your eye, or even the one up your backside. It's always the same. You can be certain it will do a better job of it than you can."

He sat back looking smug.

Callum's dad spoke. "Uncle Alexander's right. If you need to discover what's going on in the world, you ask the device and the Foxbook tells you. What you're suggesting is that we go around choosing our own news. Where would we end up if we did that? It just doesn't make any sense."

Callum's mum nodded.

"And if you to choose to go somewhere it's the Uberskyapp, if it's to know how to vote then the Borisbook tells you. It's just how the world works. Without the device we go back to the dark ages."

"And so," said his mum seriously, "to find a partner, the only thing to trust is the UgovTinder."

"Aye," said cousin Rab. "That guy from up the road, it chose him one of those nice aliens."

"And see at the tongue on her," said Uncle Thomas. "The laddie's never been happier from what I hear."

Callum's dad nodded.

"Come on, what you're suggesting is that we travel back to the days when your old grandad here was a wee lad back in the mists of time."

The old man smiled a sweet smile.

"Aye," said cousin Adam. "I was at the museum a few weeks ago and back then they had these weird things called books. They looked like they weighed a ton, and these little stick things, think they called them pens and pencils."

"Oh aye, I remember," piped up old Grandad. He had been propped up in a chair in the corner and had barely made a sound. His wizened old face became suddenly animated.

"I used to go to school, and I had to take books, and pens." He screwed up his lips looking as if he had just eaten sour lime. "Oh yes, it was terrible, terrible."

He shook his head at the memory.

"Such an inconvenience. The things we put up with in the olden days." His eyes seemed to mist over as he reminisced. "Even had to drive our own cars, and travel to these places called shops when we wanted something. There were no drones, so we had to carry stuff home ourselves in bags."

Cousin Ralph looked stunned at this revelation while Adam's narrow eyes widened with disbelief.

"We even had to wipe our own bums," said Grandad grimacing.

"Yuck," said cousin Margery with a look of disgust.

"Mingin'," said cousin Rab looking like he might gag.

At this point Callum realised he was fighting a losing battle. He decided it best to shut up and refuse to say anything more on the subject. He stood and retired to the loo.

It was cooler than the packed living room, a low whirr as his shirt changed temperature to compensate. He looked out from their high vantage point over the river. It was quiet. Other than the gentle whine from the unmanned security boat nothing was moving. Only the two swans gliding through the light purple tint on the water as it made its way to the Firth. On the other side, three seagulls squabbled with a scruffy looking drone, the new automated boat yard whirred and clanked. Its huge robotic arms secured and spray painted one of the wings on the sleek silver sky yacht that was taking shape in the dock.

Och, thought Callum, *maybe they are right.*

*

Afternoon moved into the evening. The windows rattled as a brief sandstorm passed through. Wine flowed, and between them they also managed to empty several bottles of whisky and ginvod. Many topics came and went among the constant babble. The invasion of Australia. The expected arrival of Covid 98. The plan for the seventh Forth Bridge. Hibernian finishing second in the premiership for the third year running. Once again narrowly pipped by the mighty Cowdenbeath from the metropolis across the Firth. They moved onto the recent executions, and then the latest ridiculous fashions.

"That bubble thing, it makes you appear as if you are not wearing any clothes at all. It's outrageous what these young folks do nowadays!" screeched Aunt Esmerelda.

"But mum it's so cooluber," Margery had protested. Everyone saw from her expression that on this occasion Aunt Esmerelda had put her foot down.

The last few rays of sun broke through and gleamed bright on the river before darkness slowly started to fall. By now Uncle Nicholas had gone beyond merry and he swayed as he pulled himself out of his chair. He stood up straight and raised his glass.

Everyone made an attempt to stand. Cousin Marion was by now so far gone she fell back into her seat while Aunt Maggie and cousin Rab didn't even bother attempting it. Uncle Thomas meanwhile had already slipped under the table.

"To the Preston clan, we are all here," called Uncle Nicholas. "We have always been here."

"To the Preston clan," the rest of the table shouted in reply.

"Leithers forever!" shouted Uncle Nicholas at the top of his voice.

"Leithers for ever!" they shouted in unison and then together slumped back into their seats spluttering and laughing.

Preston Family

Male timeline

Peter	*b 1348*
Richard	*b 1365*
William	*b 1396*
John	*b 1450*
Thomas	*b 1491*
Fergus	*b 1531*
Son	*b 1573*
Nicholas	*b1598*
Joseph	*b 1621*
Rab	*b 1651*
Edward	*b 1680*
Samuel	*b 1704*
Adam	*b 1724*
Ralph	*b 1750*
Alexander	*b 1778*
Isaac	*b 1838*
Frank	*b 1879*
Johnny	*b 1902*
George	*b 1925*
Billy	*b 1956*
Gabriel	*b 1999*

The Author

William Haddow was born and has spent much of his life in Edinburgh (though a foreigner to Leith, having been brought up in Meadowbank/Portobello.) A retired social worker, "Leithers" is his first novel. As well as writing he spends his time on golf, motorbikes, playing in a country music band, his allotment and as an unpaid domestic servant.

Printed in Great Britain
by Amazon

47316041R00149